AN INTEGRAL GUIDE TO
RECOVERY

Twelve Steps and Beyond

Guy du Plessis

Published by Integral Publishers
http://www.integralpublishers.com
4845 E. 2nd St.
Tucson, AZ 85711
831 333-9200

ISBN: 978-0-9904419-5-3

Cover design: QT Punque

Our printer certifies the following:
- All wood product components used in black & white, standard color, or select color paperback books, utilizing either cream or white bookblock paper, that are manufactured in the LaVergne, Tennessee Production Center are Sustainable Forestry Initiative® (SFI®) Certified Sourcing.
- All wood product components used in black & white, standard color, or select color paperback books, utilizing either cream or white bookblock paper that are manufactured the Allentown, Pennsylvania Production center are Sustainable Forestry Initiative® (SFI®) Certified Sourcing.
- The cream or white bookblock paper in black & white, standard color, or select color hardcover books manufactured in the LaVergne, Tennessee Production Center or the Allentown, Pennsylvania Production Center is Sustainable Forestry Initiative® (SFI®) Certified Sourcing.
- All wood product components used in black & white or standard color paperback books, utilizing either cream or white bookblock paper, or premium color paperbacks on white bookblock paper, that are manufactured in the Milton Keynes UK Production Center are Forest Stewardship Council® (FSC®) Mix Credit. FSC® C084699

Easy is the descent to the Lower World; but, to retrace your steps and to escape to the upper air—this is the task, this is the toil.

~ Virgil

CONTENTS

ILLUSTRATIONS

FOREWORD

Addiction is a form of human struggle that requires us to stay honest, humble, and open-minded. When a client comes to my therapy office who is facing addiction, I know from years of experience that it will take real effort to uncover the full scope of his or her story. I can't rely on only one theory or set of questions; I will need to consider every dimension of the client's life. If I don't, I will certainly miss something crucial to their recovery. This isn't only my personal perspective. Psychologists simply do not know what ultimately causes, defines, or most effectively treats addition. Those who tell you they do are either overconfident or are overstating the facts.

In terms of causes, we have some evidence that genetic inheritance, personality traits, underlying mental illnesses, gender, exposure to early trauma, lack of social support, age-of-first-usage, family-of-origin issues, and socioeconomic and cultural conditions all can contribute to addiction. But what we cannot say ahead of time is whether any of these given factors will play a role in creating a specific person's addiction. We are even farther away from understanding how combinations of these factors interplay and reinforce each other in addiction.

What's more, we know that addiction is not really a single, identical condition. Instead it is a family of conditions having to do with a mixture of compulsive behavior, emotional suffering, and physiological dependency. Some addicts turn to drugs, others to alcohol, some to gambling, sex, eating, and so on. Some use incredible quantities of their drug-of-choice and their life stops functioning altogether. Others use less and keep their life afloat, however precariously. There is a dizzying variety of addictions. That said, the most bewildering question of all may be treatment. Don't hear me wrong. Much of what we do to help addicts truly does work. We can say, generally speaking, that in order to become and stay sober from a serious addiction, almost everyone will need to develop strong motivation, social support, a new set of behaviors, some form of spirituality (whether that includes a defined god or not), the ability to think rationally and realistically, and capture therapeutic insight into childhood. But there is no single way to meet these goals that works for everybody. Every person's treatment is like a magical concoction with different ingredients that must be brewed specific to that person.

All of these reasons point to why an Integral approach to treating addiction is so very important. The Integral approach captures all the ways that professionals, researchers, and the recovering population think about the causes and possible ways of treating addiction. Integral includes the psychological, the spiritual, the genetic, and the social (and more). It does so without arguing that one is more important than another—it starts from the presumption that they are all equally important. Integral is *radically inclusive*.

In this book, Guy du Plessis does a wonderful job of contributing an Integral perspective to the 12-step traditions—the oldest and certainly among the most powerful ways to treat addiction. For those of you deeply involved in the 12-step traditions, you should take heart and know that adding an Integral lens does nothing to alter the core identity of the Twelve Steps. In fact, not only are Integral and 12-step traditions compatible, they are deeply aligned in their essences. Without taking anything away from the tradition itself, Integral is able to add key insights and practices that can have lifelong benefits for each of us. We all need help. Even our best traditions and paths, if we think about them this way, can use a helping hand now and then. We simply have to be humble in the face of problems that have moved beyond our control. Integral can help each of us struggling with addiction achieve a more comprehensive recovery and a fuller life well into recovery. Integral broadens that path for each of us.

I invite you to enter this journey with Mr. Du Plessis whether you are in recovery yourself or a person who works with others struggling with addiction. This book is highly accessible but never simplistic. It will be immensely beneficial for lay people and professionals alike. Many professionals such as myself feel that Integral is the future of mental health treatment, as do many clients who have been exposed. Stay with the lessons of Integral until they start to sink in and inform how you approach addiction. In your author, you have one of the true pioneers and best guides in how to bring Integral into our healing. He has lived it himself, and he has put it into practice with others. Use this book to broaden your horizons and open up whole new dimensions in what you thought recovery could be and how you can assist others with it.

Sincerely,

Mark Forman, PhD

Licensed Psychologist

Author, *A Guide to Integral Psychotherapy*

ACKNOWLEDGEMENTS

As with many books, this book would not have been written without the assistance, support, and inspiration of many people. The ideas and contents of this book developed over the last twenty-five years of my life, which I divide into three stages: my own experience of addiction, my personal recovery, and finally, working as an addiction treatment professional. Each of these stages of my life and the people I met in them contributed to this book in a unique way.

It is only through experiencing the horrors of addiction that I have had the impetus to write this book—the main reason for it being that some of the most amazing people I have ever met, and am likely to meet, were many of the addicts I got to know and love while in active addiction. In particular, the heroin sub-culture of Cape Town in the early and middle 1990s. I found it tragic that these amazing, yet lost, souls with so much potential were dying and withering away. In those days, I promised myself that if I made it out of addiction alive, I would dedicate a significant portion of my life to try and help people like them.

Without the love and support of many in my personal recovery, I would not be alive to write this. Arie, for phoning my father and convincing him to send me to rehab; my father, for sending me to treatment; Gareth, my first counselor; Eros and Russell (RIP), who offered me an extra two months treatment for free and took me back after a relapse; my friend, Deon (RIP), who helped me laugh myself better through treatment and made me realize the most essential elements of successful recovery— friendship, meaning, and having fun; Brad, "The Bullet," my first band member in recovery, who gave me the opportunity of dreaming about being a rock star; David, one of my first and most enduring friends in recovery; Alwin, my oldest and best friend, who stuck by me through it all; my sponsors, Peter H. (RIP) and Guy M. And a special thanks to Ingrid for her belief in me, and Peter B. for helping me through a particularly difficult period in my recovery and a special thanks to my "mothers" Debbie and Prue.

In the context of my professional life, the team at Tabankulu Secondary, who were my first "test pilots" of the early development of the Integrated Recovery approach, especially Spencer Hill, as well as Hugh Robinson (RIP), who allowed me the creative freedom (against all better judgment) to design and implement this approach at his business. A special thanks to my friend and colleague and Integral Recovery pioneer, John Dupuy, for all his support and love, as well as his wife, Pam. Without his encouragement, I would not have started this book. A shout out to Dr. Peter Nielsen for his painstaking editing work on an early draft of this text and encouragement. Thanks to Millie for graphic design and support. Thank you to Andre Marquis for feedback on this manuscript and encouragement. Thank you to Lynwood Lord and Sean Esbjörn-Hargens for all their assistance while publishing my articles at the JITP. To Dr. Mark Forman for the eloquent forward to this book, and for his support. To Heidi Mitchell for the meticulous final editing. And Dr. Bob Weathers for his support and friendship and for enduring my "epistemological-ontological" ramblings. Gratitude to Dr. Stanley Block for his support and input in the sections of my book that deal with his work. Thank you to my teacher Michael Mugaku Zimmerman for all the support and wisdom, and his wife, the amazing Diane Hamilton. Thank you to Jeannie Carlisle, Keith Bellamy, and Russ Volckmann of Integral Publishers for believing in this book. Finally, a tremendous amount of gratitude to Ken Wilber for his support of my book and articles, and for just being who he is—without the inspiration of his work, this book and approach would not be possible.

A big thanks to some of my intellectual and philosophical heroes who have inspired me over the years, who have all contributed to this book in some manner: Friedrich Nietzsche, Albert Camus, Jan Smuts, Carl Jung, Gautama Buddha, Colin Wilson, Medard Boss, Martin Heidegger, Hermann Hesse, and my father, Lindsay du Plessis.

Finally, to my utmost inspiration, my beloved daughter Coco, who helped me find my heart, and who daily shows me the wonder of "being-in-the-world."

PREFACE

It seems I was destined to face the nemesis of addiction. A week before my fourth birthday, my mother committed suicide by taking a drug overdose. She was an addict who, at the time, could not see any other way out of the devastation that addiction caused in her life. My mother was the first of many people in my life that I would lose to the disease of addiction.

In the early morning hours, my mother's sister, Christine, fell asleep in her car while driving home after a night out in Cape Town. On the final bend of the coastal road to Hout Bay, she had a head-on collision with a 21-year-old man, on his way to work on a movie set. Both died. I was living with Christine and her ten-year-old daughter at the time. Christine had struggled with drug addiction since her modeling days in Europe.

My dear friend Cecily was murdered on her way to score cocaine in Hillbrow, Johannesburg. The police found her body discarded on the side of a road. She was killed by an addict, who had tried to steal a large sum of money paid to her by the Road Accident Fund. She had waited for years for that money and used to talk about what she would do with it when she got it. She had it for only a week. Cecily had had a long battle with alcoholism and cocaine addiction.

My beloved and best friend of 14 years, Jurie, died of a "heart attack" at the age of 32. His mother found his dead body in their family house in Stellenbosch. They found used heroin syringes in his cupboard. Jurie was the most benevolent and the kindest soul I've ever known. He was also the best poet I ever encountered. Both of us had long battles with heroin addiction.

My ex-girlfriend and cherished friend, Natasha, who loved Dostoyevsky and Tom Waits so much, died from a heroin overdose—four days before she was booked to go to rehab. She battled with alcoholism and heroin addiction for over 16 years. Natasha was a superbly talented sculptor and artist, as well as a prolific writer, and left behind thousands of pages of writing. She was the first girl I ever fell in love with.

My friend Deon was found dead in his car shortly after leaving rehab. He, too, died from a "heart attack." Deon spent most of his adult life in rehabs and that was where we became friends. He struggled with codeine and crack addiction since the age of 18. He was 38 when he died, and he left behind his wife and two-year-old daughter.

Many of the people whom I spent time with while in active heroin addiction have passed away. To the world, they are merely statistics in some research report on drug abuse in South Africa in the 1990's—statistics now locked away in a moldy room—but I remember them as unique and amazing individuals.

Beautiful Minette with her long, black hair committed suicide after years of heroin addiction and prostitution. She was only 24 when she took her life.

Mark, the artist and fire blower, had a drug-induced heart attack after an all-night crack binge in the hippie commune where he lived, in Brixton, Johannesburg.

Storm left behind two kids when she died from a heroin overdose; but actually, she died much earlier—after years of prostituting herself on Sea Point's main road to support her heroin habit. You could see it in her eyes.

Shelly, the stripper, died from a Pinks (Wellconal) overdose in the arms of her husband, Steward. He was the one who had injected her with Pinks.[1] Steward died later from a heroin overdose, after his last failed attempt at rehab. His brother also died, many years before he did, from a drug overdose. Their mother lost both her sons to drugs and is looking after Steward and Shelly's child.

Mike, the soft-spoken and proficient bass guitarist, who played in many of the underground bands in Cape Town in the early 90s, died from an opiate withdrawal complication after many years of battling with heroin addiction.

Nina eventually died from a drug overdose. She had heart problems from years of injecting Pinks. I remember how a concerned and well-meaning doctor in Somerset West used to check her heart before he gave her a prescription of Pinks. I also remember how one night she was crying and begging my friend Kader to help her find a "working" vein before the Pinks and blood congealed in her syringe. They tried in her feet and her underarms, but all her veins were collapsed after years of injecting.

Marius, or as he was commonly known, "Phale," used to make beautifully grotesque clothes and poetry books from the inner-tubes of car tires. He died from a Pinks overdose after battling with Pinks and alcohol addiction for years.

If we want to include the addiction to cigarette smoking here, then I have to add my grandfather, who died from emphysema, to the list; and my father, who died from lung cancer.

What deeply saddens me about the above-mentioned deaths—apart from the obvious tragedy of the waste of human life and the loss of those I loved—is that these people were some of the kindest, most intelligent, sensitive, beautiful, and talented individuals I have ever met. This is the real sadness of addiction: it often destroys the best of us. Like canaries in a coal mine, the most sensitive die first. Society often tends to see addicts as congenitally inferior human beings. In many cases, I believe the exact opposite is true. Due to their other-worldly sensitivity, they are often the most susceptible to the pathologies of society. Did their punishment fit their "crime?" Philip K. Dick says the following about his fellow drug users, in his novel *A Scanner Darkly*, a semi-autobiographical sci-fi about drug abuse, "They wanted to have a good time, but they were like children playing in the street; they could see one after another of them being killed—run over, maimed, destroyed—but they continued to play anyhow. We really all were very happy for a while… but it was for such a terribly brief time, and then the punishment was beyond belief: even when we could see it, we could not believe it."[2]

I believe addiction is one of the many consequences of a dysfunctional society—the sicker the society, the greater the number of its sensitive souls who will become sick. The only true, lasting "cure" for addiction is not to go to war against it, although this might be part of the solution, but for humans to evolve as a society and a species.[3] What our planet needs right now are more people waking up—more people collectively contributing to the conscious evolution of our species. Collectively, as a human race, we need to "internally transform" from our fragmented ego and ethnocentric stage to more worldcentric stages of collective consciousness in order for our species to survive, for it "is the only stance that can freely, even eagerly, embrace global solutions."[4]

Although addicts can be seen as a consequence of a dysfunctional society, ironically, recovering addicts can be part of the solution towards a more functional society. I believe the recovery communities, numbering in the hundreds of thousands all over the world, can play a significant role in the evolution of our species, because, in a nutshell, recovery is the process of the evolution of our consciousness. All the millions of recovering addicts on the planet—all who are evolving—are greatly contributing to the collective state of our species' consciousness. Moreover, each one is affecting the consciousness of those they come across, a living example of the message they are carrying. You are not just recovering for yourself but for all mankind! Just think of the difference we are making and can still make.

Until we evolve adequately as a society and as a species, addiction will remain an enormous problem in the world, and some of the finest of us will keep on dying. And until then, books like this one will be necessary—books that attempt to address the problem of addiction by providing a possible solution for those who seek it.

This book is dedicated to my fallen comrades: Cecily, Jurie, Natasha, Deon, Nina, Phale, Mark, Storm, Shelly, Mike, Steward, Minette, Christine, and to my mother—and all the other sensitive souls that have paid the ultimate price for the developmental and evolutionary failures of the human race.

INTRODUCTION

*A hero ventures forth from the world of
common day into a region of supernatural
wonder: fabulous forces are there encountered
and a decisive victory is won: the hero comes
back from this mysterious adventure with the
power to bestow boons on his fellow man.*
~ *Joseph Campbell*

In the information age of the 21st century, the world has become exceedingly complex. Never before in history have we had access to the sum total of all human knowledge, technology, and wisdom. If you are engaged in a recovery process from addiction, this has two significant consequences. First, it has become increasingly difficult to navigate and make sense of the world and our place in it. Second, as a recovering addict you have virtually unlimited access to an abundance of psycho-spiritual technology to augment your personal recovery. Consequently, finding the right path and methods to recovery can often be perplexing to the newcomer as well as the "old timer."

This book presents to you the recovering addict a progressive recovery map and toolkit suitable for the complexities of today's world. This ultra-modern approach to recovery is known as Integrated Recovery. Integrated Recovery is a truly holistic lifestyle approach that provides all the essential structure and knowledge to guide you in working a wholly comprehensive, inclusive, and sustainable recovery program, achieved through an integration of the best contemporary knowledge and personal development tools. Although Integrated Recovery is a novel approach, it has not set out to reinvent the wheel as such, but is a synergistic framework that includes many time-honored recovery practices. As a holistic framework, Integrated Recovery is an approach that attempts to include and honor all the vital aspects of our lives in a comprehensive way. The Integrated Recovery approach breaks the dichotomy between living one's life and having a recovery program; this approach creates an Integrated Recovery Lifestyle that embraces all the dimensions of one's life.

Integrated Recovery is a 12-step, abstinence-based approach that is informed by Integral Theory, mindfulness, positive psychology, and existentialism. The reason I use the word "Integrated" to describe this approach is because it integrates your recovery program and your life; moreover, this approach is an integration of many disciplines. I use the word "Recovery" from two perspectives: the first is the conventional perspective that you are "recovering" from addiction; the second is that you are "recovering" and moving towards your True Self. One perspective is about moving away from—the other is about moving towards. And one process is driven by emptiness—and the other by abundance. The Integrated Recovery approach honors both of these processes. I believe both of these movements are essential aspects of the recovery process.

The aim of the Integrated Recovery approach is essentially twofold: to arrest any addictive behavior and to develop an Integrated Recovery Lifestyle that enables you to strive towards your full potential and satisfy your various innate needs as a unique human being. There are two central premises behind Integrated Recovery theory. The first is that addiction affects all the fundamental aspects of our existence and therefore, for recovery to be optimally effective, it should include practices that stimulate healing and growth in all the same areas. The second premise is that addiction is the pathological manifestation of the frustration of our inherent human need for wholeness, belonging, meaning, as well as many other innate needs. Simply put, drug abuse and addiction can be understood as a dysfunctional method that individuals apply to try to get their needs met, and to fix any unmet needs (pun intended). In short, the fundamental aim of this book and the Integrated Recovery process is to assist you in finding healthy and sustainable means to satisfy these innate needs.

Just Another "Holistic" Approach?

What makes the Integrated Recovery approach unique, relative to other holistic and integrative approaches to recovery, is that it implements the revolutionary ideas of the Integral model, as originally developed by the American philosopher Ken Wilber.

The word "integral" means comprehensive, inclusive, and non-marginalizing. The Integral model, or Integral Theory, attempts exactly that: to include as many perspectives and methodologies as possible within a coherent view of any topic. The Integral model is capable of helping to design a "recovery worldview" that allows a truly holistic approach to recovery and its practices. As a result of its all-inclusive nature, Integral Theory is currently being applied in 35 academic and professional fields, such as psychology, ecology, organizational and business management, advertising, politics, art, and law—and recently in the context of addiction and recovery.[5] The Integrated Recovery approach is part of the nascent but rapidly developing field of Integral Addiction Treatment. Integral Addiction Treatment is an umbrella term that refers to addiction treatment and recovery approaches that apply Integral Theory.

To those of you who are in a 12-step fellowship, the Integrated Recovery approach does not change anything about the Twelve Steps or its culture; it merely reframes it within the context of an inclusive and comprehensive worldview. It is like having stronger headlights on your car when driving—the Integral map does not change the territory, but it illuminates more of it, thereby giving you more informed choices. So, an Integrated Recovery Lifestyle is one that includes a traditional 12-step recovery program but also addresses many other essential areas of being human. According to this "wider" definition of recovery, there is no significant aspect of our lives that is not considered part of recovery. Recovery becomes a lifestyle without boundaries between recovery and life. What makes this approach different from traditional approaches to recovery is that the latter normally refer to a recovery program that only includes a 12-step program or psycho-therapeutic activities, whereas an Integrated Recovery Lifestyle includes and transcends a 12-step program and conventional therapy—extending to all essential areas of our lives.

The Integrated Recovery approach is not a substitute for 12-step fellowship literature or participation but an adjunct. I want to make this point very clear, as I know many people in recovery are skeptical of anything that is not strictly Twelve Steps. In many ways this is justified, as a lot of other approaches to recovery, particularly the ones devised by some academics and medical experts, are so far removed from the reality of recovery and addiction that many of their methods are more often than not ineffective and unsustainable. One only has to look at some of the early psychoanalytic theories of addiction to see some misguided efforts at explaining addiction.[6] Unfortunately, this healthy skepticism often goes to extremes; any statement about addiction and recovery made by someone who is not part of a 12-step fellowship will frequently be disregarded as uninformed and inaccurate. This extreme approach is very counterproductive. The founding fathers of the Twelve Steps never claimed that their original text was meant to be the final and ultimate authority on alcoholism or addiction. This sentiment is made clear in the *Big Book* of AA: "Our book is meant to be suggestive only. We realize we know only a little." Moreover, AA's philosophy originally came into existence as a synergy of many disciplines and diverse influences, including the ideas of the pioneering psychiatrist Carl Jung and American philosopher William James.

I believe the Twelve Steps of AA, and its fellowship, was, at its core, an attempt at an integral approach to treatment for alcoholism. It is actually amazing how forward-thinking and pluralistic the original ideas of AA were, considering they originated in the pre-Second World War era of the 1930s. So if you are reading this and thinking this book is about an alternative to the Twelve Steps—something that you have been successfully applying in your life—don't worry, it's not. The Integrated Recovery approach does not attempt to replace or substitute anything about the Twelve Steps, but rather gives you the capacity to apply it even more effectively. If you are skeptical, that is good. We should all be skeptical, as there are a lot of "false prophets" in the world today, and around every corner there's a self-help guru who claims to know the ultimate method to happiness. Yet I ask you to heed the words of philosopher Herbert Spencer, as quoted in the *Big Book* of AA, "There is a principle which is a bar against all information, which is proof against all argument, and which cannot fail to keep a man in everlasting ignorance—that is the principle of contempt prior to investigation."[7]

Purpose, Structure, and Limitations

Recovery is all about action—no action, no recovery. And not just any action—the right action. To adopt an Integrated Recovery Lifestyle, you need to learn how to work and internalize an Integrated Recovery Program. This book is dedicated exclusively to showing you how to design, plan, and execute your own personalized Integrated Recovery Program. We are all unique; therefore our recovery paths will also be unique. One size recovery does not fit all. This book will help you find a recovery program that is best suited to your unique needs. I need to warn you at the outset—you are required to do the work. Reading this book will not give you recovery, but merely inform you what to do. If you thought this would be a quick fix or a silver bullet, unfortunately, this it is not.

Many of you reading this are between a rock and a hard place—either the hard work of recovery or the hard work of active addiction. As you know, and contrary to popular belief, addiction is very hard work. Actually, I think addiction is harder work than recovery—at least for me it was. The difference is that the hard work of addiction leads to misery and eventual destruction, whereas the hard work of recovery leads to more freedom and happiness. Addiction and recovery share the common denominator of hard work but have radically different outcomes. So your reality is this: you have hard work to do either way, the choice lies in the outcome you desire—misery and destruction, or freedom and happiness.

This book is written specifically for those of you in recovery or new to recovery. It is not an academic evaluation of addiction or recovery, or a manual for therapists (I will be publishing a manual for therapists related to this approach).[8] This book's aim is to provide an outline of a functional map and toolkit for your recovery journey. It will assist you in designing your own personalized Integrated Recovery Program, which can be defined as mindfully practicing your physical, psychological, intellectual, existential, social, and environmental dimensions as part of an Integrated Recovery Lifestyle that is geared towards continued personal growth in relation to self, others, and your being-in-the-world.

Furthermore, this book is not designed to replace the work that is typically needed for individuals in early recovery. It is primarily intended for individuals who are stabilized in their recovery and have worked through their denial system and for "old timers" who need some additional guidance, as there is very little literature available for individuals who have been in recovery for several years. Although the framework of this approach is neutral in the sense that any practices the individual chooses can become part of their recovery program, I have intentionally included the philosophy and suggestions of 12-step programs, for reasons that will become more apparent later in the text. Finally, this book does not claim to have all the answers or to be an authoritative text on recovery, it is merely a particular approach to recovery that some clinicians and individuals in recovery have found useful.

Chapters one and two explore the core influences and philosophies that inspire the Integrated Recovery approach, providing brief overviews of Integral Theory, mindfulness, positive psychology, existentialism, and 12-step philosophy. In the remaining chapters, which cover the practical application of the Integrated Recovery approach, I introduce the various practices, in each of the six recovery dimensions (physical, psychological, intellectual, existential, social, and environmental) that form part of an Integrated Recovery Lifestyle, and explain how all of these practices work together synergistically. I'd like to remind the reader that this book does not provide an exhaustive discussion of all aspects of a recovery lifestyle, but it does offer an introduction and initial foundation for each of the recovery dimension outlined. The chapters on the recovery dimensions end with suggestions and written excercises that will assist you in designing your recovery practices for that recovery dimension. Chapter nine will assist you in putting together your own personalized Integrated Recovery Program.

Recovery as the Hero's Journey

In his seminal book *The Hero with a Thousand Faces*, the widely influential philosopher Joseph Campbell describes a common pattern found in all hero myths. Despite variations among the myths, Campbell identifies a similar heroic mythic structure shared by all: the hero's departure, an initiation and transformation by great trials, and the hero's return with his newfound treasure or wisdom. By juxtaposing recovery from addiction with the stages of the hero's journey, it becomes apparent that the path of recovery, as with all great adventures, follows a pattern similar to this timeless mythic structure. There are thousands of people whose recovery stories bear a striking resemblance to Campbell's hero's myth.

This book is a supportive travel companion for those on a "heroic journey of recovery"—from the clutches of addiction to healing and ultimately to wholeness. The Integrated Recovery approach will provide you with a detailed map and the necessary tools for your own heroic journey, by utilizing cutting-edge recovery and personal development technologies in synergy with the collective experiential wisdom of millions of "recovery heroes" who have been on this noble quest before you. If you are new to recovery, give it a try—it may just be one of the greatest adventures of your life.

CHAPTER 1
THE INTEGRAL MAP

If you are trying to fly over the Rocky Mountains, the more accurate a map you have, the less likely you will crash. An Integral approach ensures that you are utilizing the full range of resources for any situation, with a greater likelihood of success.

~ Ken Wilber

As recovering addicts, it is often the case that when we enter a recovery process via 12-step fellowships or formal treatment, we may feel overwhelmed by the large amount of novel information and skills we have to acquire and practice. Moreover, trying to make sense of the world in the current information age, with its multitude of often conflicting spiritual, religious, political, and psychological disciplines and worldviews is confusing and disheartening for many. The Integrated Recovery approach addresses these issues.

In 12-step fellowships, there are various slogans like "Keep it Simple." What is meant by these slogans is that the practices that are initially needed to clean up are fairly straightforward and common knowledge within fellowship culture, i.e., work the steps, do service, and go to meetings. It is true that we need to keep our lives and recovery practices fairly simple initially. It is also true that recovery is a multi-dimensional, multi-layered, and multifarious process. Just like if we were shot with an arrow, we wouldn't need to understand why or who shot us before we pulled out the arrow, we are initially encouraged to perform the practices without necessarily understanding why and how they work. While keeping the folk wisdom of recovery culture in mind, it is also true that we need a certain level of cognitive insight into the nature of both the problem and the solution for recovery to be sustainable. This is regardless of what recovery level you are at and particularly true for high-altitude recovery. It is also true that there is, as with any skill, a baseline of simplicity and practice that one cannot drop below before it becomes ineffective. The Integrated Recovery approach is about finding the simplest and most effective solution to a complex problem. It can do this because it uses the Integral map.

Why an Integral Map?

When you travel into unknown territory you need an accurate map. The Integral map is thought to be one of the most accurate maps of reality currently available. If you, like me, find recovery a complex and often confusing process, you might find the Integral map as useful as I do in illuminating the recovery process. As mentioned already, the Integral model, or Integral Theory, is a philosophical framework initially developed by Ken Wilber; it now also includes the influence of many other scholars and researchers. The aim of Integral Theory is to provide a comprehensive and inclusive conceptual framework for any phenomenon that it is applied to. Integral Theory by itself is not a simple model, but when applied to any field, it actually simplifies one's understanding of it. This is because the model increases one's range of perception of the territory, thereby providing a big picture that holds together all the many threads. When Integral Theory is applied in the context of recovery, although there is initially more information to ingest, it actually makes the recovery process easier to understand and practice, in the same way a detailed map, although it contains more information than a simpler one, makes navigation and understanding of the territory easier and more effective.

Dr. Andre Marquis, a pioneer in Integral Psychotherapy, states, "Integral Theory is a way of knowing that helps one strive for the most comprehensive understanding of any phenomenon"[9]— in our case, recovery from addiction. If our aim is to find a model to use as a framework to support a truly comprehensive and effective holistic approach to recovery, it seems that Integral Theory is best suited for the task. In the following discussion, I provide an overview of the essential elements of Integral Theory, indicate how they inform the Integrated Recovery approach, and point out how an understanding of these elements can help you to gain a more comprehensive understanding of your recovery process and practice.[10]

The AQAL Model

Integral Theory is also known as the AQAL model, referring to the five elements of Integral Theory: all quadrants, all stages, all lines, all states, and all types. I will use the terms Integral Theory, Integral map, and the AQAL model interchangeably, as they all refer to the same model. In Integral Theory, the five perspectives or elements mentioned above denote the most basic patterns of reality. By including all of these perspectives in any situation, you are ensured of not neglecting any aspect of the situation or event you are investigating. By using the AQAL map in the context of addiction and recovery, you are provided with what many consider the most comprehensive and inclusive conceptual map of human potential thus far developed. Let's start our discussion of Integral Theory by exploring what Wilber refers to as the "quadrants."

Quadrants

Sean Esbjörn-Hargens, a leading Integral scholar-practitioner, says "[according] to Integral Theory, there are at least four irreducible perspectives (subjective, inter-subjective, objective, and inter-objective), four modes of being-in-the-world, that must be consulted when attempting to fully understand an issue or aspect of reality. Thus, the quadrants express the simple recognition that everything can be viewed from two fundamental distinctions: 1) an inside and outside perspective, and 2) a singular and plural perspective."[11] The quadrants are not merely abstract constructs of reality but are also part of the very essence of your "being-in-the-world" in the here and now; you can actually feel every one of these perspectives. They are the "I," "We," "It," and "Its" (or 1st person, 2nd person and 3rd person) pronouns, which the languages from all cultures possess—because they point to the reality of each moment. These four perspectives and ways of being are always present in each moment, whether we choose to acknowledge them or not.

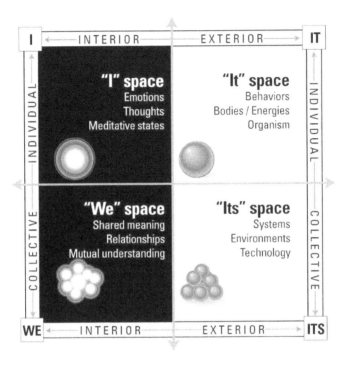

Figure 1: Four Quadrants of Integral Theory[12]

Addiction & Recovery Viewed Through the Lens of Each Quadrant

Let's take a brief look at addiction and recovery by viewing them through the quadrants or "lenses" of the AQAL model. I hope to show you succinctly that treatment of addiction, or a recovery program, that does not incorporate all these perspectives will, by default, be partial. I will also show you why it is necessary to include practices in each of the four quadrants as part of your Integrated Recovery Lifestyle, in order for it to be sustainable.

The "It" of Addiction and Recovery

Understanding addiction and recovery by exploring objective characteristics of an individual—from an Upper-Right quadrant perspective (the "It" space)—requires that we include all the observable "outside" aspects of the individual. From the viewpoint of this quadrant, addiction is often classified as a "brain disease." Addiction affects the mesolimbic system of the brain, which is the area of the brain that houses our instinctual drives as well as our aptitude to experience emotions and pleasure. This part of the brain includes the medial forebrain bundle, popularly known as the "pleasure pathway." The chronic use of drugs and/or compulsive addictive behavior "hijacks" the pleasure pathway of the brain. The resulting neurochemical dysfunction causes the individual to perceive the drug as a life-supporting necessity similar to breathing, drinking, and eating. In spite of the adverse consequences of addiction, this clarifies why most addicts cannot stop on their own, but require external support. Although I share the opinion that addiction has a strong physiological aspect, I do not see addiction as merely a "brain disease;" it is much more complex than mere dysfunction of neurophysiology.[13]

In the treatment of addictions and maintenance of recovery, many emphasize the importance of diet and nutritional supplements. Some believe that most addicts suffer from reward deficiency, which is a neurochemical imbalance in the brain specifically related to our capacity to experience pleasure and positive feelings. This neurochemical imbalance in brain chemistry results in negative effects, including feelings of emptiness, hypersensitivity, and anxiety. Even prior to the onset of active addiction, some individuals may have deficiencies in brain chemistry.[14] In addition to long-term use of mood-altering substances, many factors can create "reward deficient" brain chemistry. Among these are genetics, prenatal conditioning, malnutrition, stress, lack of sleep, and physical or emotional trauma. Unless rectified, brain chemistry deficiency continues indefinitely into an addict's recovery. This means that recovering addicts remain prone to relapse, even if they are abstinent and doing psycho-spiritual work. Only after the neurochemical imbalance is corrected will symptoms of reward deficiency abate.

Some researchers argue that effective treatment requires a combined physiological and psychological approach as well as improving an addict's neurophysiology.[15] Physical and neurological health is vital for an effective addiction treatment program and sustainable recovery. In this area of recovery, our health is fueled by exercise, diet, supplements, sleep, limited or no caffeine intake, and various physiologically oriented therapies.

The "I" of Addiction and Recovery

From the perspective of the Upper-Left quadrant (the "I" space), an exploration of addiction and recovery includes the subjective or the "inside" experience of an individual's consciousness. Addiction wreaks havoc in the addict's inner world with negative consequences cognitively, existentially, and emotionally. The addict loses control over his/her inner world as the "addict voice" becomes progressively "louder." Developmentally, addicts often regress to egocentric and childlike states of self-centeredness and unreasonableness. Addiction develops from a definite, but often seemingly indistinct, beginning to a specific end point—the end point being the complete control of the self by the illness.

This quadrant of recovery receives a considerable amount of attention in most reputable addiction treatment approaches. Psycho-spiritual healing is achieved through therapeutic practices like 12-step work, psychotherapy, lectures, trauma counseling, meditation, and individual therapy. Recovery processes that exclude cognitive, emotional, existential, and spiritual healing, as well as education, are partial and ineffective in providing sustainable sobriety. An essential feature of treatment is cognitive insight into the nature of addiction and recovery. Becoming familiar with the basic elements of the Integral map provides us with a "meta-recovery structure" that illuminates the whole recovery process.

By tradition, and as a result of AA's influence on addiction treatment, spirituality is considered an essential element in effective treatment protocol. Through Integral Theory, treatment providers and recovering addicts gain a more complete understanding of spirituality and spiritual methodologies. According to AA, addiction results from a lack of spirituality. Spiritual practices play an important existential role in "healing" addiction, because they provide a sense of meaning to life that is often lacking in the addict population. Neurotheology researcher Michael Winkelman argues that spiritual practices can also free addicts from ego-bound emotions and provide balance in contradictory internal energies. A sense of "wholeness" can be achieved through spiritual practices, which counteracts the sense of self loss that is at the core of addictive dynamics.

The "We" of Addiction & Recovery

Developing an understanding of addiction and recovery from the Lower-Left quadrant perspective (the "We" space) includes one's cultural and interpersonal aspects. While addiction is often caused by eroded relationships, it also progressively erodes relationships. Because addicts are often unable to form healthy intimate relationships, addiction is commonly seen as an intimacy disorder or attachment disorder.[16] Family and friends may be perplexed and outraged as the addict's behavior progressively transgresses the cultural norms that are held by family, friends, and colleagues. Many addicts undergo a cultural shift and eventually enter the "world of addiction" that has its own rules and cultural norms. Here, addictive behaviors are accepted and often encouraged, and addicts are given a new set of culturally relevant information as well as a new set of rules. Author and addiction recovery researcher William White writes that "[w]hat begins as a person-drug relationship moves toward an all-encompassing lifestyle. No part of the persona is left untouched by the culture of addiction."[17]

Many of us find that these cultural and relational aspects of addiction are the hardest to give up. Non-users find it difficult to understand the thrill, meaning, brotherhood, and "adventure" provided by addiction—at least while the going is good. Eventually, addiction destroys all the supposed benefits of the addiction culture, but often the addict continues searching in vain for those early carefree days that are like a tantalizing mirage, always out of reach. Writing on heroin addiction, novelist William Burroughs says: "Junk is not just a habit. It is a way of life. When you give up junk, you give up a way of life."[18] It is the illusion that certain "fun" aspects of this way of life can be re-lived that draws many addicts back to it. Treatment that does not acknowledge and understand the ideology behind the culture of addiction, and the need for a healthy recovery culture, is likely to be ineffective. White goes on to say that "[a]ddiction and recovery are more than something that happens inside someone. Each involves deep human needs in interaction with a social environment. For addicts, addiction provides a valued cocoon where these needs can be, and historically have been, met. No treatment can be successful if it doesn't offer a pathway to meet those same needs and provide an alternative social world that has perceived value and meaning."[19]

I believe that correct cultural association is one of the key remedial aspects of the recovery process, particularly in early recovery. The central reason the 12-step methods are so successful is because the recovery neophyte is introduced to established recovery cultures that provide an immediate sense of acceptance and belonging. Not many people understand the sense of belonging provided by certain drug cultures. Most aspects of the "straight world"—its social clubs, religions, and institutions—are sorely lacking in comparison with the camaraderie and intimacy of some drug cultures. A cold, aloof, and intellectually-based recovery culture cannot compete with that.

Luigi Zoja, past president of the International Association of Jungian Psychoanalysts and renowned author, believes that the pervasive use of drugs in our society can be ascribed, to a large extent, to the revival of a collective need for ritual and initiation. A longing for the sacred underlies the ritualized world of addiction. Often addiction is not an escape from the world but a desperate attempt to find some sense of belonging. A successful recovery culture should provide new healthy rites of passage. The "chip," or key-ring, that addicts receive on their milestones in Narcotics

Anonymous (NA) meetings may satisfy, to some extent, deep, archetypal human needs. These tokens function as "symbols of initiation" and are often proudly displayed. A pivotal aspect of any recovery structure is to provide access to a supportive and informed recovery community—one that provides new and healthy cultural norms, a sense of belonging, and support.[20]

The "Its" of Addiction & Recovery

Exploring addiction and recovery from the Lower-Right quadrant perspective (the "Its" space), we include the observable aspects of societies, such as their economic structures, civic resources, and geopolitical infrastructures. Addiction affects this realm profoundly, and this is especially true for those addicted to "hard drugs," like crack and heroin. Drugs are expensive. Addicts often lose their jobs, get evicted, get into trouble with the law, and are sometimes incarcerated. As is said in NA, the result of addiction is "jails, institutions, and death." There are many acultural and bi-cultural addicts who manage to stay employed and have financial stability, but for most addicts, this quadrant is severely compromised. The culture of addiction's infrastructure includes crack houses, bars, night clubs, casinos, strip clubs, areas of prostitution, and so on. Progressively, addicts move from one culture to another and begin to spend more and more time within the infrastructure of addiction culture. The more complete this migration becomes, the more resolutely it normalizes their behavior, which ultimately reinforces their denial of the problem of addiction.

The addict enters recovery through treatment, therapy, or 12-step programs, and in doing so, enters the infrastructure of recovery. It is vital that the beginner avoid dangerous "people, places, and things," and the entire infrastructure of addiction in which his addictive behavior is welcomed and reinforced. This NA folk wisdom becomes obvious when viewed from the "Its" space perspective. An effective recovery program must address this area at the outset, by providing a new infrastructure that deals with legal, monetary, and accommodation issues.

A sustainable discharge plan concerning this dimension of recovery is an absolute necessity. Recovering addicts in 12-step fellowships seldom consider their education, legal, monetary, residential, or administrative aspects as a fundamental part of their recovery. Financial and administrative unmanageability can be serious stumbling blocks to psycho-spiritual well-being; the distress of unmanageability in these areas has caused many addicts to relapse. Healthy participation in recovery infrastructure and financial and administrative manageability are strongly promoted and advocated by the Integrated Recovery approach.

Recovery: An All-quadrant Affair

Our brief look at the four quadrants of addiction and recovery shows clearly that addiction affects all the quadrants of an addict's life and that they are all interconnected. We cannot meaningfully address any one quadrant without including the perspectives of the other three. Out of necessity, recovery presupposes health and stability in all quadrants, and that pathology in one area will negatively affect all the other areas. As with the human body, if one organ is not functioning optimally, then the whole system suffers or dies.

Determining the essentials in providing a sustainable recovery lies at the core of the Integrated Recovery approach. An

Integrated Recovery Program ensures that you are covering all your bases, and that no areas are overlooked that might weaken your whole recovery system. All systems have vital limits, and systems theory states that by removing any essential part, the system collapses. Fire, for example, is a simple system that requires three vital elements to function: heat, fuel, and oxygen. Fire dies by removing any one of its three elements. All fire-fighting theories are based on this principle. Although it is a complex system, recovery is governed by the same set of laws. When any of the essential elements are removed, the system is weakened and as a result, can collapse.

Lines of Development

Each facet of reality, represented by the four quadrants, has individual capacities or "multiple intelligences,"[21] which develop independently from one another and continually advance or regress. These are referred to as lines of development, or simply "lines." Each quadrant comprises many lines of development, for example, the individual-interior quadrant of experience includes cognitive, emotional, spiritual, moral, interpersonal, as well as many other lines identified by Wilber and other developmental theorists. It is likely that you are well developed in some lines and less so in others. For example, you may be well developed along the cognitive line while lacking in interpersonal growth. Through an understanding of lines, we realize that different aspects of ourselves are at different levels of development.

In the context of recovery, this is a crucial insight. Certain aspects of our recovery are likely to be more advanced than others. Furthermore, if certain aspects of your recovery are poorly developed, then these aspects may jeopardize your entire recovery process. The Integrated Recovery approach identifies six essential lines of development, referred to as the six recovery dimensions: physical, intellectual, psychological, existential, social, and environmental. These six recovery dimensions cover the major areas of the quadrants in the context of recovery and are fundamental to an Integrated Recovery Lifestyle. They represent six always-present modes of being-in-the-world.

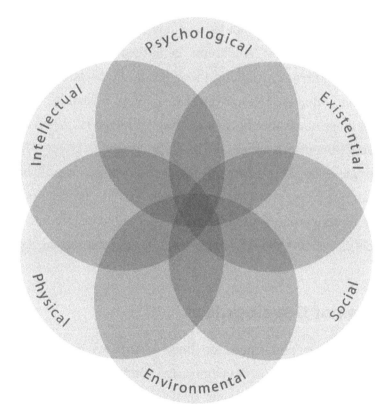

Figure 2: Six Recovery Dimensions or Modes of Being-in-the-World

As with lines, each of the six recovery dimensions can be at different stages of development for individuals in recovery. Unless these six recovery dimensions are functioning at a reasonable level of development, the whole system is in jeopardy. Acknowledging that we need to practice our physical, intellectual, social, psychological, existential, social, and environmental dimensions will not suffice. Action is required to bring each dimension to a minimum level of development before the whole system can be considered healthy.

Each recovery dimension signifies a cluster of needs, highlighting our needs in a certain area of our life and the inescapable, existential fact that, as humans, we must have these needs met somehow. Addiction is a dysfunctional and non-sustainable attempt at having these needs met, whereas a well-developed Integrated Recovery Lifestyle is a healthy way of having these needs met in each recovery dimension. When all six recovery dimensions are plotted on an Integrated Recovery Graph, it provides you with a graphic illustration of the overall health of your recovery process. This simple graphic presentation of your recovery process provides easily accessible insight into what aspects can and/or should be improved. I will return to this later.[22]

Stages of Development

Each recovery dimension, or line, progresses and fluctuates through a sequence of developmental altitudes that, in Integral Theory, is referred to as stages, or levels of development. Wilber states that "stages" of development are also referred to as "levels" of development, the idea being that each stage represents a level of organization, or a level of complexity.[23] An insight into addiction and recovery from a stage perspective is imperative for a truly all-inclusive understanding. As my colleague John Dupuy, author of the book *Integral Recovery,* says, "recovering addicts find learning vertical development theory instructive and inspirational. Knowing that you are aspiring to a higher version of yourself provides a meaningful direction for your recovery process."[24]

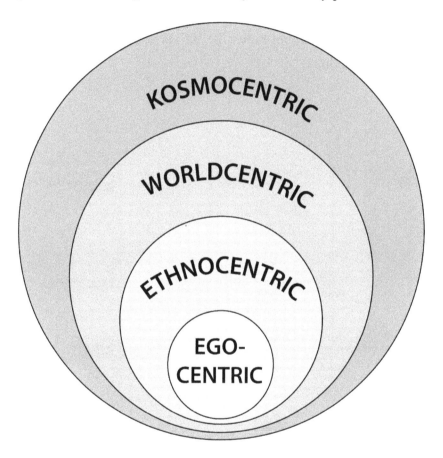

Figure 3: Moral Stages of Development[25]

From a moral developmental perspective, an easy way to understand stages is to describe their progression from egocentric through ethnocentric to worldcentric. All of us grow through these stages and different "intelligences," or lines of development. Any parent, or anyone that has observed children growing up, knows how extremely self-centered young children are, and that they will gradually develop a greater capacity to recognize the feelings and needs of those around them. The recovery dimensions of our Integrated Lifestyle progress or regress according to the amount of effort we put into each of these areas. Nobody can play guitar the first time around, but rather the skill is acquired as more time is spent practicing.

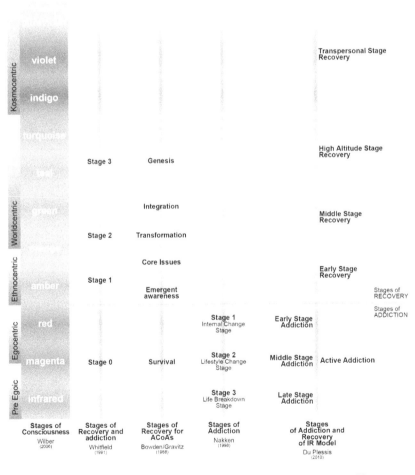

Figure 4: Stages of Addiction and Recovery[26]

In the figure *Stages of Addiction and Recovery,* I indicate Wilber's developmental model on the left, and to the right of that, various developmental models of addiction and recovery, including my own composite developmental model relating to addiction and recovery. This figure shows the various developmental stages that our center of "recovery gravity" can possibly rest at, and how it may correlate with general psychological development.[27]

Through an understanding of a developmental approach to addiction and recovery, we expand our insight into the nature of addiction, and more importantly, we develop a conceptual map of our recovery path. We learn how addiction stops personal development and, in many cases, causes developmental deterioration to lower, egocentric levels. This explains why we display such self-centered behavior in active addiction, because we regress to a level of consciousness that has little regard for others. We can also see that our recovery will be at different levels of development at different points in time, and that at each developmental stage, we require a new set of "recovery skills" to function satisfactorily. This is an important insight for recovery pilgrims: for continued growth, you must exert effort throughout your journey of recovery. What worked for you in the past might not apply today, in the same way that the skills used to pass Grade 1 mathematics will not be adequate to pass Grade 10. This phenomenon is true for all facets of life and most certainly for the recovery process. Many recovering addicts believe that the program they worked when two years clean will work when they are ten years clean—a common fallacy among those in recovery. I must add that this does not mean that we should discard the initial practices, but rather that we need to continuously add to the existing practices.

The stages of recovery that I indicate on the far right in the figure *Stages of Addiction and Recovery* can be understood in the following way. Early stage recovery refers to the stage where the focus is on abstinence and relapse prevention. Middle stage recovery is where the focus is on working through various psychological issues, family of origin issues, and behavior patterns that often predated the onset of addiction. In this stage of recovery, many addicts also begin to work on co-dependency issues, relationship issues, and behavioral addictions, which tend to surface once the substance dependence has been arrested.

High altitude stage recovery is perhaps best understood as an existentially-oriented stage, where the recovering addict is faced with life and social concerns that transcend addiction and conventional definitions of recovery, and also transcend concerns about oneself. This is a stage that most people enter (whether they are recovered from an addiction or not), when they have done a significant amount of introspection, therapy, study, and/ or contemplative practice. At this stage, the distinction between addict and non-addict begins to fall away. A "recovery lifestyle" will share similarities with the lifestyle of any individual at a similar stage of development. This is also the stage where the concept of fellowship begins to have a much more inclusive scope than merely 12-step fellowships.

Not all recovering addicts will naturally progress into a high altitude stage of recovery by default of staying clean. Many of those in recovery seem to stay in a middle stage of recovery, where they remain preoccupied with themselves and their personal issues and problems. The transpersonal stage of recovery can be understood as a stage that requires a special type of practice and orientation to attain, whereas the earlier stages are characterized by building ego strength and developing a relatively well-integrated sense of self. The transpersonal stage aims at transcending the ego and sense of self. This developmental stage of recovery is normally reserved for those that have engaged in a significant amount of Eastern or Western contemplative practices.

With knowledge of the various stages available to us in recovery, we recognize the fact that at each stage of the recovery process, we will view ourselves and our relationship with the world in a different way. Advancing through the stages of recovery requires that our Integrated Recovery Program become increasingly sophisticated in order to remain optimally successful. This suggests that the vague notion of "serenity" used in 12-step fellowships is often misleading, because each new stage presents new difficulties and struggles. This is not to say that one does not become more "serene" with development, but rather that each stage of recovery has its own struggles and challenges. After many years clean, addicts in late recovery are often puzzled when they find themselves in psychological turmoil. This is frequently mistaken to mean that they are not working the fundamentals of their program. Sometimes this may be the case, but more often, it results from the fact that they have entered a new recovery stage and are confronted with new challenges. Returning to basics is not always the answer. Instead, the basics are included and augmented with practices relevant to the new recovery stage.

On the one hand, addiction is characterized by constricted awareness, which results in low developmental altitude, and on the other hand, recovery is characterized by an increase in awareness, which is accompanied by an increase in developmental altitude. Ultimately, the Integrated Recovery approach aims to promote your overall vertical development by including practices that stimulate growth and awareness in all six recovery dimensions of your Integrated Recovery Lifestyle.

States of Consciousness

Regardless of our stage of development, various states of consciousness are available to us. Addicts are experts on states. Using substances—or any mind-altering behavior—is an attempt to create an altered state of consciousness, and various drugs correlate with various types of altered states. Researchers argue that the majority of addiction treatment programs fail to integrate the huge body of literature that highlights the therapeutic benefits for addicts of experiencing altered states of consciousness (ASC). They propose that a principle reason for the high relapse rate in treatment programs is the failure of those programs to address the basic need to achieve ASC and to provide addicts with healthy ways of doing so.[28] Some argue that humans have an innate drive to seek ASC.[29] From this viewpoint, drug use and addiction are not understood as an intrinsic anomaly, but rather as a yearning for an inherent human need. Winkelman states that "[t]his near-universality of institutionalization of ASC induction practices reflects human psychobiological needs. Since contemporary Indo–European societies lack legitimate institutionalized procedures for accessing ASCs, they tend to be sought and utilized in deleterious and self-destructive patterns—alcoholism, tobacco abuse, and illicit substance dependence. Since ASC reflect underlying psychobiological structures and innate needs, when societies fail to provide legitimate procedures for accessing these conditions, they are sought through other means."[30]

A brief example of this premise, which highlights our need for altered states, is the work of Harvey Milkman and Stanley Sunderwirth in their book *Craving for Ecstasy and Natural Highs*. "In light of the seemingly universal need to seek out altered states, it behooves researchers, educators, parents, politicians, public health administrators, and treatment practitioners to promote healthy means to alter brain chemistry."[31] Addicts have found a way to have this need met through substances or certain behaviors to which they have become addicted. Addicts normally have three dominant ways of seeking comfort, satiation, arousal, and fantasy, and these preferred styles of coping might already be present in the first years of life. Milkman and Sunderwirth go on to say that "[c]hildhood experiences combined with genetic predisposition are the foundations of adult compulsions. The drug group of choice—depressants, stimulants, or hallucinogens—is the one that best fits the individual's characteristic way of coping with stress or feelings of unworthiness. People do not become addicted to drugs or mood-altering substances as such, but rather to satiation, arousal, or fantasy experiences that can be achieved through them."[32]

AA acknowledges the importance of an alteration of consciousness for recovery to be effective; it calls for "a new state of consciousness and being,"[33] designed to replace the self-destructive pursuit of alcohol-induced states with a healthier, life-enhancing approach. AA advocates meditation, a change in consciousness, and spiritual awakening as fundamental to achieving and maintaining abstinence. For these reasons, the Integrated Recovery approach advocates healthy, non-invasive, life supporting practices and therapies that encourage alteration of consciousness.

Types

Knowledge of "types," or typologies, is essential to a comprehensive understanding of addiction and recovery. "Types are the variety of consistent styles that arise in various domains and occur irrespective of developmental levels. As with the other elements, types have expression in all four quadrants."[34] It follows that, in each of the four quadrants, we can have a variety of classifications of different types in the context of addiction and recovery. These include, but are not restricted to, types of addictions (heroin, crack, etc.), types of cultural enmeshment (a-cultural, bi-cultural, and culturally enmeshed), types of dual-diagnosis, types of "kinship" in sub-cultures (punk, metal, trance, hip hop, criminal, etc.), "brain state" types, and DSM-IV-TR axis II disorder types.

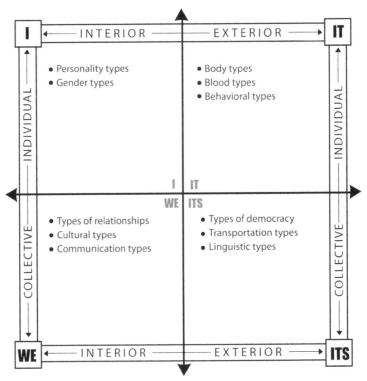

Figure 5: Types in All Quadrants[35]

There are many personality types in the context of addiction and recovery. One example is that of feminine and masculine types. "When we speak of 'masculine' and 'feminine,' we are not necessarily speaking of a biological 'male' or 'female.' Rather, we are referring to a spectrum of attitudes, behaviors, cognitive styles, and emotional energies."[36] In my opinion, the psychoactive properties of drugs, as well as aspects of process addictions, can include a masculine and/or feminine "voice." "Downers," like tranquilizers, barbiturates, and heroin, can be said to have a feminine "voice." In addition, addictions like co-dependency, love addiction, certain behaviors of sex addiction, and certain aspects of gambling (particularly slot machines) have a similar voice. On the other hand, "uppers," like cocaine, methamphetamine, and process addictions, such as certain high-risk aspects of sex addiction and gambling (especially those who play tables), represent a more masculine "voice."

I believe that these masculine or feminine "voices" of specific addictions are likely to correlate with specific "addiction neuropathways." "Masculine addictions" trigger the "arousal neuropathways" of the brain—these are about pleasure and intensity. "Feminine addictions" stimulate the "numbing or satiety neuropathways" of the brain that produce a calming, relaxing, and soothing effect. I have also observed a connection between the object-relations (referring to internalized patterns of relationships) that addicts have with their parents and their drug(s) of choice. I believe that addicts' "object-relations" can have pathological masculine and/or feminine aspects. As a result, an individual's brain chemistry becomes more prone to certain masculine or feminine addictions, the purpose of which is to rectify the neurochemical malfunctions caused by dysfunctional relationship patterns. This could explain why many heroin addicts have distant or absent fathers and are enmeshed with their mothers. In contrast with this, many cocaine addicts tend to have distant or absent mothers and authoritarian fathers. Interestingly, I have also observed that when addicts "cross-addict"—moving from one addiction to another—they are inclined to remain within masculine or feminine addiction types. From this perspective then, addiction can be seen as a dysfunctional attempt to rectify the addict's pathological masculine and feminine relationship patterns. If not treated, the addict will seek to cure such imbalances by dysfunctional means.

Because of the above, understanding the "voice" of the addiction can help in choosing a suitable therapeutic treatment plan. Many addictions and addiction systems can only survive in the dialectic between masculine and feminine "voices;" for example, between the alcoholic and the co-dependent enabler, or the "dance" of the love addict and the love avoidant. To return this to a healthy balance, one must identify which "voice" has become pathological.

Let's use the heroin addict as an example. S/he is addicted to a "feminine" drug, and there are few things in the world that instantly soothe and "nurture" like a shot of heroin. Evidently the heroin addict needs self-soothing and nurturing—possibly due to being enmeshed with an over-involved mother or a distant/absent mother. Consequently, the addict never learns how to self-soothe, nurture, and take care of him or herself. This may manifest itself in areas like administrative unmanageability (common among heroin addicts). This may also explain why heroin addicts are known to enter relationships in early treatment and often have love addiction traits (a feminine-voice addiction). The heroin addict has unresolved nurturing and self-soothing needs, and if not taught how to satisfy these needs in a healthy way, then s/he will continue to cross-addict.

An understanding of the masculine and feminine voices of our addiction can guide us in recovery, because it can point out our individual needs. We can understand the "masculine addiction" as agency gone awry, and "feminine addiction" as communion gone off-center. Those driven by unhealthy agency need balancing through healthier agency, while those driven by unhealthy communion need balancing through healthier communion.[37] It follows that understanding types of addicts in recovery can be a very helpful resource. Appreciating the characteristics of various types that you exhibit—personality types, brainwave state types, neurological constitution types, and so forth—will help identify your particular requirements and alert you to the specific features that your Integrated Recovery Lifestyle must include.

The Integral Operating System

As we reach the end of this introduction to Integral Theory in the context of addiction and recovery, it should be obvious to you by now that an understanding and application of Integral Theory is a very useful model for those working a recovery program. Integral Theory is often compared to the operating system of a personal computer. Running Windows 8 on your computer instead of MS DOS enables your computer to run and perform more complex tasks and software. In the same way, Integral Theory, once "installed," alters and upgrades your whole body-mind system. Integral Theory is psychoactive; once "ingested," it alters your system permanently. "The result is that any brain hardware system operating on IOS [Integral Operating System] automatically scans all phenomena, interior as well as exterior, for any quadrants, waves, streams, or states that are not being included in awareness,"[38] thereby increasing the scope of your "recovery awareness." The AQAL model augments your consciousness, enabling you to navigate your life with bigger and stronger headlights, illuminating more of your internal and external realities.

CHAPTER 2
FOUNDATIONAL INFLUENCES

Now that we have explored the Integral map in relation to the Integrated Recovery approach, let's look at some of the other principal foundational influences of this approach, namely: mindfulness, positive psychology, existentialism, and the Twelve Steps. Although Integrated Recovery is influenced directly or indirectly by several therapeutic and philosophical orientations, the ones discussed in this chapter (alongside Integral Theory) provide the foundation and conceptual scaffolding of this approach to recovery. Each of the perspectives and methods of the various approaches discussed in this chapter, when placed within an Integral framework, synergistically provide a robust recovery worldview to base your recovery process on.

Mindfulness

The secret of health for both mind and body
is not to mourn for the past, nor worry about
the future, but to live in the present
moment wisely and earnestly.
~ Shakyamuni Buddha

In 12-step fellowships, members are advised to live "Just for Today." This simple yet profound slogan can be seen decorating the walls of thousands of 12-step meeting venues all over the world. For newcomers to 12-step fellowships, heeding the counsel of this slogan is what keeps many alive in the painful early days of withdrawal, with their customary feelings of hopelessness. Experienced sponsors tell newcomers to stay clean "just for today" not to worry about tomorrow, only to make it through today without using. Most of us in early recovery find the prospect of never using again an unfathomable concept—but can tolerate the idea of not using or drinking for 24 hours. As we make it through the stormy early days of recovery, we start to see that the concept "Just for Today" is applicable to all life situations. Living "Just for Today," or living "Just for the Moment," profoundly changes the experience of any given situation. We come to learn what suffering "projecting into the future" and "regretting the past" hold, and what joy and freedom are to be found living in the Now.

Think back to some of the happiest moments in your life. What these moments most likely had in common, apart from the fact that they were memorable and pleasant, is that you were there. Now that seems like an obvious and even silly statement; what I mean by being "there" is that you were being truly present in that situation. When we think about many of our life situations, we find that we might be there in body, but in our minds, we are elsewhere. We are either worrying about our future, thinking about the past, or daydreaming some fantasy, pleasant or unpleasant. I venture to say that we are very seldom present. Then, there are moments in our lives when, due to some set of circumstances, we are really there—watching a beautiful sunset, seeing our child being born, surfing the perfect wave, and so on.

When we are truly happy in our surroundings, we are always present. The rest of the time, we are on automatic pilot, and unfortunately our automatic pilot follows a route that is often negative. Think of all the negative thoughts that arise in your awareness daily; they are automatic and are the consequence of all of your previous experience and conditioning. If you were raised in a dysfunctional family and society, then your programming will likely be dysfunctional in many ways, and your automatic pilot will use an inaccurate and ultimately destructive map. A term used to describe this state of being present in the now is mindfulness. Many therapeutic practices that apply the concept of mindfulness can be very useful for those in recovery.

Mindfulness is the state we are in when we experience a situation mostly free from our past conditioning. All truly beautiful and great moments are moments of mindfulness. As Jon Kabat-Zinn, developer of the Mindfulness-Based Stress Reduction Program, describes, "Mindfulness is an ancient Buddhist practice which has profound relevance for our present-day lives. This relevance has nothing to do with Buddhism per se or with becoming a Buddhist, but has everything to do with waking up and living in harmony with oneself and with the world. It has to do with examining who we are, with questioning our view of the world and our place in it, and with cultivating some appreciation for the fullness of each moment we are alive. Most of all, it has to do with being in touch."[39]

Developer of the Mind-Body Bridging method (MBB), Stanley Block ascribes collapsed awareness as the root of addiction—or any dysfunction. Denial, which is one of the primary obstacles to recovery, is, in essence, a profound narrowing of awareness. This in turn leads to a fragmented understanding of the damages done by and the reality of one's addiction, which perpetuates the addictive cycle. The practice of mindfulness can be seen as an awareness-raising activity, which can have immense benefits for those of us in recovery.

As identified in our discussion of states, it is imperative that treatment programs provide accessible and healthy opportunities for Altered States of Consciousness (ASC) for their clients. Mindfulness meditation is an example of such a practice. Practices like mindfulness meditation that produce healthy ASC also have many physiological benefits for addicted populations. Researchers have proposed a neuroendocrine model for the mechanisms by which meditation reduces addiction. The ability meditation has to reduce stress and enhance serotonin functioning addresses the dysfunction of addiction on a physiological level.[40]

As Fritz Perls, co-founder of Gestalt Therapy, writes, "Without awareness there is no cognition of choice."[41] With awareness, there is choice and consequently, for the addict, the ability to break the cycle of addiction. Perls believed that, in and of itself, awareness is curative. Much of his Gestalt Therapy was aimed, therefore, at helping individuals bring awareness to areas of themselves they were not fully conscious of. He stated that if a patient "can become truly aware at every instant of himself and his actions on whatever level—fantasy, verbal, or physical—he can see how he is producing his difficulties, he can see what his present difficulties are, and he can help himself to solve them in the present, in the here and now."[42] Wilber believes that the theme of awareness being curative runs through virtually all psychotherapeutic theories, as it does in Gestalt Therapy. It is curative for a central reason: by bringing awareness to parts of our psyches, we begin to experience them as objects, and this allows us to differentiate and transcend them.

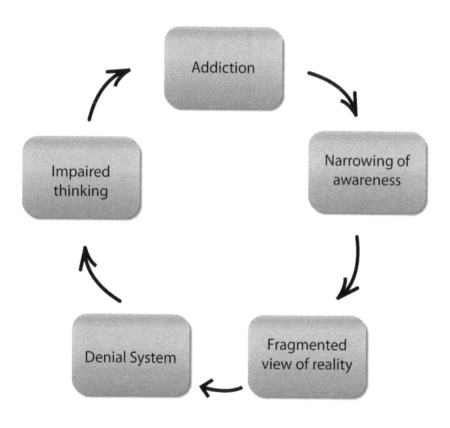

Figure 6: Cycle of Addiction[43]

When we have unmet needs, they take the foreground of our awareness until they are met; our awareness narrows to find ways to have those needs met. Addiction can be understood as one ever-present "unmet need." When addicted, our awareness remains narrow to find ways to meet this persistent (and impossible to satisfy) need. Buddhists have an apt metaphor for this, referred to as a "hungry ghost;" no matter how much you eat, the food just falls straight through you. After years of this "narrowing of awareness," our awareness may become permanently constricted, thereby perpetuating the addiction cycle by not allowing the full spectrum of reality to enter our restricted awareness. This becomes fertile ground for an elaborate denial system, based on a fragmented view of our reality, and explains why what is obvious to others is not always obvious to the addict. Consequently, the raising or expansion of awareness is imperative for sustainable recovery.

Mindfulness Meditation

In the Eleventh Step, it is advised that we pursue some form of meditative practice. The term meditation is often used very broadly within 12-step culture, which is in keeping with its pluralistic philosophy. The downside of this is that people often have "meditative" practices that by any conventional definition would not even remotely be considered meditation. In the NA basic text, there are the following general guidelines: "So our preliminary practice is aimed at stilling the mind, and letting the thoughts that arise die a natural death. We leave our thoughts behind as the meditation part of the Eleventh Step becomes a reality for us."[44]

The guidelines of NA's basic text echo the guidelines of many formal meditative practices. It should be clear that these guidelines do not point to relaxation exercises or idle daydreaming but to some form of meditative practice—the primary aim of which is to still the mind. True stillness of the mind can only be achieved by the practice of proper and habitual meditative exercises. Ken Wilber and developmental psychologist Robert Kegan believe that meditation significantly increases awareness and this in turn promotes vertical personal development. This is because when we meditate, the subjects of our current awareness become the objects of awareness at the next level of development. In meditation, and especially in mindfulness meditation, we merely observe our experiences as they unfold. Therefore, over time, we gain some objectivity about them, and consequently they have less power over us, providing us with the opportunity to acknowledge them in our decisions but not be overpowered by them.

Jungian analyst Walter Odanjnyk proposes a theory in which the benefits of meditation lie in the act of concentration. He states that during meditation, psychic energy is withdrawn from its habitual flow among our instincts, drives, fantasies, thoughts, feelings, and complexes. The energy we put into ego defenses, personas, and so on, is transferred to our efforts of concentration. He believes that the transformational effects of meditation are due to consciously focusing the mind on the object of meditation, thereby altering the natural, habitual flow of psychic energy. Through meditation, the individual gradually starves and shrinks the drive complexes, and in the case of addiction, the dysfunctional addictive part of the addict's personality.

Most addicts would agree that we suffer from overactive minds and that most of our psychic energy is taken up by what is known in recovery culture as "stinking thinking;" in other words, thinking which is negative, counterproductive, and based mostly on irrational fears. It therefore makes sense that those of us in recovery would benefit tremendously from meditation that provides some reprieve from a mind that is normally conditioned in a multitude of dysfunctional ways of perceiving the world. From an Eleventh-step perspective, we can say that when the habitual "stinking thinking" abates, conscious contact between the individual and a Higher Consciousness, or Higher Power, is strengthened.[45]

Mindfulness is about waking up and being fully with whatever is in the here and now. As Kabat-Zinn points out, "wherever you go, there you are," and whatever is happening is happening—regardless of your desires. The only truly sane way to deal with reality is an attitude of presence and acceptance; any other method will keep us asleep and ignorant. Block states that, "Trauma not only energizes requirements of living the past, but also causes the system to generate new requirements of dyspresence; a need to avoid being present in the moment."[46]

When we truly live "Just for Today," we are alive in present reality, which for the most part is experienced as a joyous event—as most of our suffering and anguish is either in the perception of past or future. Through mindfulness, we maintain a "bird's eye view" of reality—we are deeply aware of life and our role in it at any given moment. This "aware attitude" leads to humility, acceptance, and gratitude. Relapse can only happen in a fragmented, narrow, and unaware state of mind. It is not difficult to see why mindfulness, as expressed in the recovery slogan "Just for Today," has become such an important and integral principle of 12-step culture. As Thoreau said, "Only that day dawns to which we are awake."[47]

Positive Psychology

Little progress can be made merely by
attempting to repress what is evil; our great
hope lies in developing what is good.
~ Calvin Coolidge

Since Aristotle, philosophers have been pondering the enigmatic questions: What is the Good Life? What is happiness? How do we achieve happiness? German philosopher Friedrich Nietzsche said this about happiness in his sublime book *Thus Spoke Zarathustra*:

> "Happiness; how little attains happiness!" Thus I spoke once and thought myself wise. But it was blasphemy: I have learned *that* now. Wise fools speak better. Precisely the least thing, the gentlest, lightest, the rustling of a lizard, a breath, a moment, a twinkling of an eye—*little* makes up the quality of the *best* happiness. Soft![48]

Like Nietzsche's sage Zarathustra, who contemplated the Good Life and the route to happiness, positive psychology is a discipline that asks and examines these same timeless questions. The Integrated Recovery approach is informed by the philosophy and methodology of positive psychology. "Positive psychology is an umbrella term for the study of positive emotions, positive character traits, and enabling institutions."[49] Positive psychology focuses on what makes people happy, as opposed to psychopathology, which is the focus of the majority of contemporary psychological approaches. Positive psychology and the philosophy of the Twelve Steps are in keeping with each other, as they both focus on increasing the quality of individuals' lives. Both focus on the solution rather than solely on the problem. The Integrated Recovery Lifestyle approach is geared to increase the happiness and quality of life of the recovering individual without dwelling excessively or exclusively on the problem of addiction or the psychodynamic roots of the disorder.

Many interventions of positive psychology are similar to those in the Twelve Steps of AA. Within 12-step fellowships, the cultivation of "spiritual principles," like honesty, gratitude, and open-mindedness, is essential. A feature of recovery is to internalize these "spiritual principles" until they are permanent character strengths. Research has shown that the practice of AA's spiritual principles is known to increase the recovering individual's chances to remain abstinent and increase their quality of life.[50] This correlates with what positive psychologists Martin Seligman and Christopher Peterson call virtues and character strengths. Integrated Recovery is informed by the twenty-four character strengths and six virtues outlined in their book *Character Strengths and Virtues: A Handbook and Classification* (CSV). Classification of the six virtues and twenty-four character strengths gives recovering addicts a structure to assess and describe their strengths. Integrated Recovery, like positive psychology, is not merely focused on fixing what is dysfunctional, but also on nurturing the positive resources of the individual.

The aim of CSV is to do for "psychological well-being what the Diagnostic and Statistical Manual of Mental Disorders (DSM) of the American Psychiatric Association does for the psychological disorders that disable human beings. The CSV describes and classifies strengths and virtues that enable human thriving. The general scheme of the CSV relies on six overarching virtues that almost every culture across the world endorses: wisdom, courage, humanity, justice, temperance, and transcendence."[51] The CSV classifies twenty-four character strengths under the six virtues.

Classification of 6 Virtues and 24 Character Strengths

1. <u>**Wisdom and knowledge:**</u> Cognitive strengths that entail the acquisition and use of knowledge.
   Creativity: Thinking of novel and productive ways to do things.
   Curiosity: Taking an interest in all of ongoing experience.
   Open-mindedness: Thinking things through and examining them from all sides.
   Love of learning: Mastering new skills, topics, and bodies of knowledge.
   Perspective: Being able to provide wise counsel to others.

2. <u>**Courage:**</u> Emotional strengths that involve the exercise of will to accomplish goals in the face of opposition, external or internal.
   Authenticity: Speaking the truth and presenting oneself in a genuine way.
   Bravery: Not shrinking from threat, challenge, difficulty, or pain.
   Persistence: Finishing what one starts.
   Zest: Approaching life with excitement and energy.

3. <u>**Humanity:**</u> Interpersonal strengths that involve "tending and befriending" others.

Kindness: Doing favors and good deeds for others.

Love: Valuing close relations with others.

Social intelligence: Being aware of the motives and feelings of self and others.

4. **Justice:** Civic strengths that underlie healthy community life.
   Fairness: Treating all people the same according to notions of fairness and justice.
   Leadership: Organizing group activities and seeing that they happen.
   Teamwork: Working well as a member of a group or team.

5. **Temperance:** Strengths that protect against excess.
   Forgiveness: Forgiving those who have done wrong.
   Modesty: Letting one's accomplishments speak for themselves.
   Prudence: Being careful about one's choices; not saying or doing things that might later be regretted.
   Self-regulation: Regulating what one feels and does.

6. **Transcendence:** Strengths that forge connections to the larger universe and provide meaning.
   Appreciation of beauty and excellence: Noticing and appreciating beauty, excellence, and/or skilled performance in all domains of life.
   Gratitude: Being aware of and thankful for the good things that happen.
   Hope: Expecting the best and working to achieve it.
   Humor: Liking to laugh and tease; bringing smiles to other people.
   Religiousness: Having coherent beliefs about the higher purpose and meaning of life.[52]

The classification of these twenty-four character strengths offers a language to describe our character strengths in recovery. In 12-step culture, both the "classification" and understanding of character defects are well established. It is as important to acknowledge our character strengths as it is to work on our character defects. Healthy functioning depends on the dialectic between our character strengths and defects. At a treatment center I use to work at, we ran a psychotherapy group exclusively dedicated to what is "right with us" and used the classification of the six virtues and twenty-four character strengths as a guideline. Additionally, we added a "Step 4 1/2 " to our normal 12-step written work. The aim of Step 4 ½ is to describe and explore how these twenty-four character strengths feature in our personality makeup, because after Step 4 (whose aim is primarily to acknowledge what is wrong in us), many of us feels like one big, walking character defect.

According to positive psychology, there are three possible routes to happiness available to us; each is different in its effect on our well-being. The first route is called the "pleasurable life." This is any activity, past, present, or future, that creates positive emotions and pleasure, i.e., eating a tasty meal, having sex, taking drugs or alcohol, daydreaming, sleeping late, buying something new, watching a movie, etc. What these activities have in common is that they all create immediate pleasure or positive effect in some way—but the pleasurable effect normally fades. Moreover, one does not need much skill to experience these states; it doesn't take much skill to eat French vanilla ice cream, and one can only eat so much before the pleasure fades.

There is nothing inherently wrong with pursuing pleasurable things in life, and they do lead to a certain degree of happiness, but as we will see, there are other more enduring and authentic ways to lasting happiness. We live in a culture where the pleasurable life is advertised daily as the only route to happiness. As recovering addicts, we know that the single-minded pursuit of pleasure does not work out that well in the end—we learned that lesson the hard way.

The second—and considerably more enduring—route to happiness is what Seligman calls the "engaged" or "good life." This includes activities that are characterized by absorption, engagement, and flow. Gratification comes about through the exercise of one's strengths and virtues. Examples of these types of activities are surfing, rock climbing, painting, playing an instrument, good conversation, and so forth. These acts may or may not include positive emotions; think of a rock climber in pain but loving the act of climbing. These activities are "earned;" they require a certain amount of skill and application of character strength, and this often creates a flow state.

Flow is a term that designates complete absorption in an experience or activity—time stops and our sense of self vanishes. Addiction is a dysfunctional way to create this flow state. Patrick Carnes, pioneer in sex addiction research, points out that for recovery to be sustainable, we need to learn new and healthy ways of accessing these flow states. He further points out that one of the reasons conventional addiction treatment approaches have such high relapse rates is that they only focus on relapse prevention and do not realize the value of focusing on one's optimum, and what a difference that can make. These gratifications of the good life lead to longer lasting and more authentic feelings of happiness, as opposed to the instant gratifications of the pleasurable life. In many ways, recovery is a movement from instant gratification to finding new gratifications based on character strengths that produce flow states.

Finally, there is the "meaningful life," which is characterized by "using your signature strengths in the service of something larger than you are." Signature strengths refer to the character assets that you display most frequently.[53] When signature strengths are applied daily, they lead to a good or engaged life, and when they are applied to something truly meaningful, it contributes to a "meaningful life."

Seligman believes that in order to live a full life, we need all three routes to happiness. In addiction, we only lived the pleasurable life and look where that got us. An Integrated Recovery Lifestyle incorporates all three routes to happiness and, according to Seligman, this will result in authentic, happy lives. To "recover" your true self and purpose, you must nurture what is "right" in you and go out there and make life happen. Merely "recovering" from addiction cannot provide you with what you want from life. As discussed above, you need to apply your character strengths as much as possible in personally meaningful pursuits. Put simply— do what you love and are good at.

My signature strengths are curiosity, love of learning, ingenuity, perspective, zest, humor, and appreciation of beauty. This is why I am writing this book—it actualizes many of these strengths—and that's why I absolutely love doing this. When I am creating something meaningful and beautiful, I am in a flow state, feeling like this is what I should be doing, and am deeply fulfilled. Learning about character strengths has assisted me to be realistic and authentic with myself and not try and be everything to all people all the time. There are many things I am really bad at, and you know what? That is just fine. So instead of torturing myself to try and be good at things I will never be good at, and perpetually lamenting my defects, I focus on what I love and am good at.

In a nutshell, happiness is... having pleasurable pursuits, applying your signature strengths at work, love, and play, and utilizing your signature strengths in the service of something greater than yourself—as part of your Integrated Recovery Lifestyle.

Existentialism

Freedom is the most ineradicable
craving of human nature.

~ Jan Smuts

One of the central philosophical foundations that informs Integrated Recovery is an existential view of human nature. Existentialism is a philosophical outlook that stresses the significance of free will, personal responsibility, and freedom of choice. This perspective emphasizes the unique experiences and needs of each individual, and the responsibility each of us have for our choices and what we make of our lives. South African philosopher and statesman Jan Smuts' theory of Holism—in its application to the human personality—is congruent with existential philosophy's emphasis on freedom. The striving towards freedom is an essential and central component of Smuts' view of human nature. He states, "[to] be a free personality represents the highest achievement of which any human being is capable. The Whole is free, and to realize wholeness or freedom (they are correlative expressions) in the smaller world of individual life represents not only the highest of which the individual is capable, but expresses also what is at once the deepest and highest in the universal movement of Holism."[54] Smuts' and the existentialist's view of freedom is a central theme that runs through the Integrated Recovery approach. Addiction can be understood as a lifestyle that severely contracts freedom, whereas a recovery lifestyle allows for a fuller expression of freedom and wholeness in our being-in-the-world.

In the context of recovery, an existential understanding would point out that we are responsible for our own recovery and how we choose to live a recovery lifestyle. We have the free will to make choices that support either a recovery lifestyle or an addictive lifestyle. The choice and the responsibility are ours alone. Even though you might have a condition that limits your free will in relation to using drugs (known as "powerlessness" in recovery circles), this does not make you powerless over the choices you have to get the right support and to follow practices that will prevent you from regressing into this "powerless" condition.

While existentialism applauds free will, it acknowledges that our free will functions within certain limitations. An important feature of living an authentic and ultimately happy life is accepting these limitations of our human nature; much of our unnecessary suffering is due to not accepting these limitations. The notion of existential limitations has many significant consequences for our understanding of addiction and recovery. In many ways, addiction can be understood as an attempt to bypass certain of our inherent limitations. While in active addiction, we try to control the uncontrollable: we attempt to avoid and medicate natural human experiences of pain, disappointment, boredom, and so forth, and stretch our control beyond its capacity. Ironically, this attempt at controlling ends up with us being more out of control—enslaved by the medium we use to try and control what ultimately cannot be controlled. Existentialism clearly articulates this dialectic between free-will and powerlessness that we have to navigate for our recovery to be sustainable.

Richard Ulman and Harry Paul, in their book *The Self Psychology of Addiction and its Treatment: Narcissus in Wonderland,* brilliantly explain how at the core of addiction dynamics, there is a narcissistic fantasy of having an unrealistic sense of control of oneself, others, and things/ events in the world. They state that "[in] the case of addiction, such a narcissistic fantasy centers on a narcissistic illusion of a megalomaniacal being that possesses magical control over psychoactive agents (things and activities). These latter entities allow for the artificial alteration of the subjective reality of one's sense of one's self and one's personal world. Under the influence of these intoxicating fantasies, an addict imagines being like a sorcerer or wizard who controls a magic wand capable of manipulating the forces of nature—and particularly the forces of human nature. Eventually, a person becomes a captive of these addictive fantasies and then becomes an addict, lost in a wonderland."[55]

From a Buddhist perspective, suffering, or dukkha, is caused by our unwillingness to accept the world as it is and our insistence on trying to make it fit our expected ideas or fantasies. Addiction is, in essence, a refusal to accept things as they are and an attempt to avoid the reality of necessary suffering at all costs. An important aspect of recovery is realizing the inevitability of suffering and learning how to cope with it in a healthy way. Happiness is earned only through hard work—not through instant gratification. "Happiness purchased cheaply is hollow and leads to little sense of mastery. Happiness attained without understanding is purchased at the price of self-respect."[56] For addicts to "grow up," they "must relinquish the paradise of limitless abundance and arrogance."[57]

Philip Flores, clinical psychologist and author of the book *Group Therapy with Addicted Populations*, sums up this existential predicament of the alcoholic by saying that "[m]any existential writers believe that in such a confrontation between the realistic acceptance of the world as it is and the self-centered demands for unlimited gratification, reason would prevail and the individual would choose more realistically between the alternatives— continued unhappy struggles with old patterns of expectations or authentic existence with expanded freedom of choice and responsible expression of drives and wishes. With Socrates, we argue to "know thyself." In this fashion, AA members are taught to believe that the authentic existence advocated by the AA program holds the key to self-examination, self-knowledge, emancipation, cure, and eventual salvation."[58]

Another feature of existentialism is its emphasis on the human condition as a whole. Existential philosopher Martin Heidegger describes human existence as *being-in-the-world* and the meaning (or meaninglessness) attached to the relationship, or rather the "interrelationship," that we have with the world. Being-in-the-world encompasses more than human consciousness; it also constitutes the fact that we exist as part of the world. This view points out that we are of the world rather than in it—we co-exist with our world. We and our experience of the world constitute an interdependent unity.

There are several important implications of such a view for understanding human nature that are relevant to recovery. For example, our environment (including other people) influences who we are, and who we are influences how we experience our environment. By placing emphasis on our being-in-the-world, existential philosophy is interested in the whole man in his relation to others and the world. Man's existence cannot be reduced to one dimension of his being. His existence is best understood as the irreducible and inseparable dimensions of feeling, thinking, and acting interdependently with others and the world. Existential man is a whole man, who includes others and the world in his wholeness.

The different recovery dimensions of the Integrated Recovery approach are strongly informed by these insights of existentialism. Each of the recovery dimensions (physical, psychological, intellectual, existential, social, and environmental) constitutes an aspect of our total being-in-the-world; they represent fundamental and irreducible aspects of our existence. We exist as these various dimensions at any given moment in time and space. When in active addiction, each of these dimensions of our being is affected, and our capacity to authentically exist in the world in each of these dimensions becomes, often severely, limited and dysfunctional. Consequently, for recovery to be sustainable, each of these areas or recovery dimensions needs to be acknowledged as essential components of a recovery lifestyle.

Moreover, as briefly mentioned already, each of these areas or recovery dimensions can be understood as representing a cluster of human needs. As humans, we have basic innate needs in each recovery dimension that can either be satisfied through healthy or unhealthy means. Very often, addiction is an attempt, albeit dysfunctional, at satisfying certain of our innate needs in one or more of these dimensions of our being-in-the-world. For recovery to be sustainable, we need to develop a lifestyle that offers us the opportunity to have our needs met in each of these recovery dimensions in healthy ways. If we don't, our addiction (when understood as a dysfunctional method of having needs met) will likely surface in that recovery dimension that is not adequately addressed in our recovery lifestyle. This is the reason this book advocates healthy practices in each recovery dimension.

In general, existentialists tend to be anti-essentialists, meaning that they believe that man has no essential nature or essence, that we exist first and then develop an essence, and that there is no universal morality. While I agree with existential thinkers like Friedrick Nietzsche and Jean-Paul Sartre that there is no transcendental universal morality, I do believe that there is an innate essence in human beings that precedes our existence. This innate or a priori essence is our basic human needs.[59] We are all born with certain psychological needs (as well as physiological) that are universal and exist relatively independently from our cultural conditioning. Moreover, these basic human needs are not merely relevant to infants and toddlers, but to all humans at any stage of life. If we have innate basic needs, this also implies an inherent morality, meaning that each person we encounter has certain needs, and our actions can either promote their needs or frustrate their needs. From an existential perspective, we could say that although we are free to make of ourselves what we want, it has to be done within the framework of our basic human needs. From an existential perspective, addiction can often be understood as a striving towards freedom, but through means that attempt to circumvent many of our inherent needs. On the other hand, an authentic recovery is the striving towards freedom that includes healthy ways to satisfy our basic human needs.

It is also important to note that the cause of addiction should not always be understood as something that was "wrong" (pathological) with an individual, and that substance abuse was an attempt to fix (pun intended) this "wrong." Sometimes the opposite can also be true: for example, the non-expression of talent can lead to addiction. Any dimension of our being that is not being fulfilled can lead to the risk of us developing some type of destructive or addictive behavior in an attempt to satisfy it. If genius, skill, or talent is not actualized or provided enough expression, due to internal or external environmental factors, it can contribute as a significant risk factor to developing an addiction disorder. For example, intelligence would normally be seen as a protective factor against addiction. But when circumstances seriously suppress the need of an individual's intelligence to find expression, then it becomes a risk factor. Simply put, being intelligent in an environment where it is not nourished becomes a risk factor for that individual, where for other people that same environment would not inhibit intellection expression or development and would thus not be a significant risk factor.

We seldom explore the existential relationship between self–actualization and environment. I have encountered many addicts who initially turned towards drugs not only because they had some deep psychological issues or trauma, but because their family or environment did not provide the means for them to find expression for their giftedness or to find adequate meaning in life. This perspective could also indicate why, among addicted populations, there are so many intelligent, sensitive, and talented individuals.

The Twelve Steps

... to learn to live and die, in order to be a
man, to refuse to be a god.
~ Albert Camus

A central feature of the Integrated Recovery approach is the philosophy and suggestions of the Twelve Steps as originated by Alcoholics Anonymous (AA). There is substantial evidence that the Twelve Steps of AA is an effective treatment modality, and a vast body of research literature substantiates this claim.[60] Furthermore, "Alcoholics Anonymous has been called the most significant phenomenon in the history of ideas in the twentieth century."[61] Research shows that 12-step affiliation buffers stress significantly, and therefore leads to an enhanced quality in the recovering person's life.[62] A longitudinal study found that AA affiliation and the application of AA-related coping skills were predictive of reduced substance abuse. The same study found a causal relationship with AA affiliation and self-efficacy, changes in social network support, and abstinence, thus expanding existing literature that suggests these same relationships.[63]

Flores believes that 12-step meetings provide identification, support, and sharing of common concerns, which are powerful curative forces. Peers are often more significant than professionals in producing behavioral change. It is imperative that individuals recover by "living in consultation" (that is, being part of a supportive and knowledgeable community), and that their recovery process is contained within a larger, supportive community. I believe that any recovery approach that does not include a supportive and informed community will generally be unsustainable. The 12-step fellowships (Alcoholics Anonymous, Narcotics Anonymous, etc.) provide extensive, easily accessible, well-established, and knowledgeable recovery communities.

There is much criticism of the Twelve Steps and its effectiveness from many individuals and organizations. In principle, I am not against any criticism of the Twelve Steps, for healthy criticism is needed for any growth process, since everything has a shadow side. Unfortunately, however, I believe that a significant percentage of criticisms of the Twelve Steps are simply misinformed. For example, the most common criticism of 12-step programs is that they promote a "theistic religious" philosophy and expect their members to believe in a supernatural God, or Higher Power. This is one example of a gross misinterpretation of 12-step programs' "pluralistic spiritual" philosophy. Twelve-step philosophy accommodates individuals with religious or secular worldviews. I find it very unfortunate that many addicts are put off by the Twelve Steps—not due to their own experience or insight—but due to others' uninformed misrepresentation of the basic tenets of the Twelve Steps. Flores says the following about the frequent misrepresentation of AA, "As far as many professionals are concerned, Alcoholics Anonymous is a much-maligned, beleaguered, and misunderstood organization. A great many of AA's critics who write disparagingly of the organization do so without the benefit of attending AA meetings or familiarizing themselves with its working on more than a passing, superficial, or purely analytical level. They fail to understand the subtleties of the AA program and often erroneously attribute qualities and characteristics to the organization that are one-dimensional and misleading and sometimes even border on slanderous."[64]

I believe most of the criticism of AA and the many other 12-step fellowships is invalid due to the perspective from which the criticism originates. The Twelve Steps is an injunctive paradigm—a set of social practices—and the only claims it makes are the likely results of following its suggested practices. To truly understand the nature of the Twelve Steps, one has to follow the three strands of valid knowledge accumulation: injunction, apprehension, and confirmation/refutation. This is where the problem originates with much of the critique of AA: to refute or validate the claims of AA, we have to follow the injunction first. It has to be "experienced," before one can confirm or refute the validity of the practice. It is an injunction that only reveals its true nature when practiced and understood from a subjective and experiential point of view.

Attempting to understand the Twelve Steps objectively, without a subjective perspective gained by following the injunctive practices, is as absurd as trying to understand Zen by reading books on Zen without any practice or direct experience. Any Zen master would tell you this is impossible, and that you are bound to make an incorrect interpretation. The same goes for any experience, like eating an apple or swimming; you can never truly understand the experience of being in the sea by reading or talking about it—only by diving into the water. Like Zen sutras, the Twelve Steps are merely the "finger pointing to the moon" and not the moon itself. Much criticism is of the finger pointing. If you confuse the map with the territory, you are in trouble.

Pragmatic philosopher John Dewey calls this type of distal knowledge "spectator knowledge." Dewey believes that authentic knowledge is only derived from the experience of the phenomenon one wants to understand. Therefore, if you want to claim any real understanding of the Twelve Steps, then "do" it—experience it—according to the suggestions. Without the "do," all consequent interpretations (whether negative or positive) will necessarily be partial and likely inaccurate and misguided.

The real and irrefutable, pragmatic proof that the Twelve Steps work lies in the millions of people, all over the world, who have followed the suggestions of 12-step programs and, as a result, transformed their lives for the better. If you are new to recovery and have reservations about the Twelve Steps, keep in mind that it has worked for millions of people just like you, and the only way you can truly have a valid opinion surrounding its effectiveness is to try it for yourself. I am certainly not of the opinion that the Twelve Steps is the only legitimate way to recovery, or that it will work for everybody, but it has worked for a lot of people, because many of its tenets are based on sound theory and practice.

CHAPTER 3
THE PHYSICAL RECOVERY DIMENSION

*It is slavery to live in the mind unless it has
become part of the body.*
~ Kahlil Gibran

Did anybody ever say to you in active addiction, "Why don't you just stop!" Sure they did. Perhaps you asked yourself this question. Why did you keep on doing things that were causing harm to you and others? It doesn't make any sense! That is exactly the point: addiction affects our brain in such a way that we "bypass" the parts that use logic and reason. Addiction affects our limbic system. The limbic system contains our brain's pleasure and reward system and concerns our survival. The limbic system "monitors the body's need for survival, and when it senses our survival is dependent on a certain behavior, it creates a compulsion so strong that it becomes extremely difficult to resist taking the action."[65] Once addicted, this part of our brain reacts to our addictive substance like it is an absolute necessity for our survival. Our limbic system interprets the absence of our addictive substance as a matter of life or death. This is one of the reasons why recovery from addiction is so difficult and cannot be cured only with good intentions. Once addicted, our brains are "wired" for addiction, and a function of recovery is the slow and painful rewiring of our brains. Because of this organic component, we need time to recover in the same way a torn muscle needs time to heal. A weekend workshop or some of your mother's tomato soup will not do.

Addiction directly affects the neurotransmitter levels of our brains. Neurotransmitters are the brain's "communication devices" and are manufactured in brain cells called neurons. Every thought, feeling, impulse, and voluntary or involuntary movement is mediated through neurotransmitter communication. Neurotransmitters play an important role in how you feel. Whether the change is brought on naturally or unnaturally, an increase or decrease in a certain neurotransmitter results in you feeling different. Addictive substances flood the brain with certain neurotransmitters, which results in a feeling of euphoria and/or relief. When you have a line of cocaine, your neurons manufacture more of a neurotransmitter called dopamine, which floods your brain, resulting in a high.

An unfortunate drawback for most addicts in their quest for perpetual euphoria is that what provided a kick last month does not work as well anymore. By the same token, a month ago a quarter gram of heroin would keep you high all day, and now you need to take a gram a day just to feel normal. Why? The brain has a built in "party-pooper" mechanism know as down-regulation. At the end of your neurons are little receptor sites where the neurotransmitters connect when communicating signals to other neurons. When your brain starts to down-regulate for a particular neurotransmitter, some of these receptor sites close and will not let the neurotransmitter dock. This means you need more of this neurotransmitter to get the same kick and consequently, you need more of the substance.

Another feature of addiction is that when you stop using, your brain has become accustomed to a certain, artificially elevated level of neurotransmitters. In the absence of the substance, the brain experiences the resulting low neurotransmitter level as withdrawal symptoms and cravings. Your limbic system interprets this as a life threatening situation—and in some addictions like alcohol, codeine, and barbiturates, it can actually be life threatening—and tends to override the logical faculties of your cerebral cortex. You feel like you desperately need this substance and will seek it out, often despite damaging consequences. You go on automatic pilot—your limbic system is driving the bus. This dysfunctional brain state has often been referred to as the "hijacked brain," and for most of us, the consequences are disastrous.

Reward Deficiency

Are you one of those people who felt whole, or felt like you "came home," when you used a certain substance for the first time? Before your addiction, were you often plagued by feelings of emptiness, low self-esteem, depression, or boredom—like something was missing? If so, you were probably reward deficient. I certainly was. When I took heroin the first time, it felt like all the pieces finally fitted, and for the first time in my life it felt like it all made sense and life was just... beautiful. That day, my reward deficient brain and I both knew that we wanted MORE.

Patrick Holford, nutritionist and author of the book *How to Quit without Feeling S**T*, explains reward deficiency as a condition where your brain manufactures too little or too much of certain neurotransmitters.[66] Your brain sends out powerful signals to rectify these imbalances, and this results in negative symptoms and constant feelings of being unsatisfied. You feel like you need something to fill the emptiness, reduce anxiety, relieve the boredom, slow down your overactive mind, or create excitement. You definitely want to feel different from how you are feeling now. Sound familiar? If you do not find healthy ways to rectify this imbalance, then you will find unhealthy ways. Note that not all addicts are reward deficient before their addiction, but will be so after quitting, at least initially, and will display abstinence symptoms. Abstinence symptoms refer to negative conditions like anxiety, poor sleep, sense of emptiness, boredom, hypersensitivity, and so on. The problem for many addicts in recovery is that they have abstinence symptoms caused by reward deficiency for years after quitting. Why? Their brains are still not producing the right amounts of certain neurotransmitters. There are many possible reasons for this. If you were reward deficient before becoming addicted, you will remain so after addiction; and even if you didn't start out being reward deficient, the neurochemical alteration that happens in active addiction has altered your brain metabolism. In either case, abstinence symptoms will most likely not abate until the neurochemical imbalance is rectified. If you are naturally reward deficient, you are more likely to become addicted, because the use of the mind-altering substance works for what ails you.

One possible cause for being reward deficient is genetics. Our genetic make-up can cause imbalances in our brain chemistry that make mood-altering substances very appealing. "Studies have shown that numerous genes are associated with conditions that manifest as symptoms of reward deficiency."[67] Genetic researchers found that people with an abnormal form of the D2 receptor genes have fewer receptors for the feel-good neurotransmitter dopamine, which renders the dopamine system ineffective. Addicts have a lower number of D2 receptor sites than are found in the average population. Further, scientists know that some alcoholics produce more of the liver enzyme called alcohol dehydrogenase II (or II ADH). This genetic predisposition causes them to metabolize acetaldehyde more slowly, which has the consequence of allowing more of it to build up in the blood stream. It seems that the very same genes that predispose reward deficiency also cause something different to happen in your brain when you use mood-altering substances. The experience for you is not merely pleasant—but exhilarating. You get even higher.[68]

Apart from a possible genetic predisposition, reward deficiency can also be the product of non-genetic causes. Prenatal conditioning, like malnutrition or the use of alcohol or drugs by the expecting mother, can result in reward deficiency. Malnutrition can result in reward deficiency, because most of our neurotransmitters are dependent on an adequate diet. Poor diet over an extended period of time may weaken the manufacturing and interaction of brain chemicals. Ongoing stress or episodes of severe stress can cause long-term damage to the reward system of the brain. Extreme stress can significantly alter brain chemistry. Lack of sleep can also significantly disrupt normal brain chemistry and cause reward deficiency. Physical trauma to the head may cause imbalanced brain neurochemistry. And finally, the heavy or long-term use of mood-altering substances can significantly alter brain chemistry. Even if you are not genetically predisposed towards reward deficiency, you may develop the condition by abusing substances.

So what is the significance of all of this in our recovery? Simply put, if we do not rectify these neurochemical imbalances, we will continue to suffer unnecessarily from abstinence symptoms, even though we are doing all the necessary psycho-spiritual work associated with optimal recovery. Reward deficiency might also be the reason why addicts tend to cross from one addiction to another. Their brains remain reward deficient, so they continue to seek ways to rectify the imbalance. It is often said in NA fellowships, "there is no chemical solution to a spiritual problem." Within our current context, I often point out that "there is also no spiritual solution to a chemical problem." If the problem is organic, or if you have a genetic predisposition, you are not going to meditate or talk your reward deficient brain back into balance. Many people in recovery seemingly do all the right things, but they remain perpetually miserable and/or unsatisfied. This is often due to the neglect of the physical recovery dimension, and consequently they continue to suffer from a reward deficient condition. This is not to say that psycho-spiritual work does not alter brain chemistry; meditation, therapy, and many other practices significantly alter brain chemistry but are limited in their effect on the brain. In the same way, nutrition can help an emotional problem, but its effects are limited in that area.

Integral Theory states that all quadrants are significant in understanding and producing change in another quadrant; but if there is a problem that is more specific to one quadrant, then you need a solution more specific to that area. Put simply, if you have a problem with reward deficiency, then you need to address this problem with appropriate practices to rectify your brain's neurochemical imbalance.

A Healthy Digestive Tract

I was surprised when I found out that our digestive tract also manufactures neurotransmitters. Half of our serotonin and melatonin is made in our gut. This brings a whole new meaning to "I have a gut feeling." Without our digestive tract working properly, we cannot extract the necessary nutrients required for our brain and body to function optimally. Many addictive substances— especially alcohol, painkillers, and heroin—damage or even shut down the digestive system and consequently, your brain and body does not receive the optimal amount of nutrients.

In early recovery, it is highly likely that your digestive tract is damaged. A healthy gut is important, because even though you improve your diet and take supplements, a damaged gut cannot adequately absorb nutrients. Therefore, healing the gut is a priority. To heal the gut, you can take digestive enzymes, glutamine powder, and probiotics. Taking a digestive enzyme complex (lipase, amylase, and protease) with meals will help to digest your food completely. With your digestive enzyme, take 10 mg zinc and 25 mg vitamin B6, since stomach acid and the protein-digesting enzymes rely on them.

Our gut's walls (mucosal cells) run on glutamine, therefore supplementing 4-8g glutamine at bedtime and again in the morning will help heal your gut's lining. Seeing that glutamine has a calming effect, it is of extra benefit at bedtime. Glutamine should not be taken if you have severe liver damage; consult a professional before commencing with glutamine supplements. Supplementing probiotics that contain beneficial bacteria such as Lactobacillus acidophilus and Bifidobacteria will help heal your digestive tract. Researchers recently found that these healthy digestive track bacteria are capable of activating neurons in the brain that make serotonin. You only have to take these gut healing supplements for about a month or two—or until you feel your digestive tract is working properly.

Vitamins and Minerals

Methylation refers to a complex process in your brain. It's like the conductor of your brain's orchestra. One of the processes for which methylation is necessary is to turn amino acids into neurotransmitters. To feel alert, happy, and connected, you need to be good at methylation—most addicts are not. It is essential in recovery, therefore, that you ensure your "methyl IQ" is high enough. To find out how high your methyl IQ is, measure the level of homocysteine in your blood. Homocysteine is an amino acid made by the body, and high levels of homocysteine mean low methyl IQ. There are many nutrients that help to lower your homocysteine level and consequently raise your methyl IQ, and the following supplements assist in raising your methyl IQ: folic acid, folate, methylfolate, vitamin B12, B6, B2, B3, magnesium, zinc, SAM, TMG, and NAC. A simple and effective way to raise your methyl IQ is to take a good quality multivitamin and mineral supplement. I suggest Solgar's *Formula VM—2000*. I also suggest a calcium and magnesium supplement at bedtime. Calcium and magnesium also help with sleep and relaxation.

Due to their bulkiness, most multivitamins do not contain the required amount of calcium and magnesium. When supplementing calcium and magnesium, take the magnesium glycinate rather than the magnesium carbonate, which is not only poorly absorbed but also neutralizes stomach acid. Greens, beans, nuts, and seeds are high in folate which lowers homocysteine levels. Coffee significantly raises your homocysteine levels. This is one of the many reasons to reduce or eliminate coffee from your diet.

Essential Fats

The use of addictive substances depletes the brain of essential fats. If you are not eating unfried, oily fish three times a week or taking daily supplements of essential fats, then chances are good that you have an imbalance or deficiency in essential fats. These fats are called essential, because your body cannot make them. The only way to obtain them is by eating them. Approximately 60 percent of the dried weight of your brain is comprised of fats—omega fats (omega-3 and omega-6), phospholipids, and cholesterol. A common source of these fats is fish, nuts, seeds, and eggs. It is of utmost importance for your brain to function optimally to have an adequate balance of these fats—your brain is totally dependent on them. These fats help with abstinence symptoms of addiction including anxiety, depression, suicidal thoughts, irritability, aggression, poor concentration, and poor memory.

Researchers found that relapse among cocaine and alcohol dependents is significantly lower for those who had an increased intake of omega-6 and omega-3 foods.[69] In this regard, there is a strong link between ADHD and addiction; the intake of essential fats improves symptoms of ADHD. Therefore, if you have ADHD or ADD, and you are in recovery, the intake of essential fats is absolutely vital. The best sources of omega fats are fish, nuts, and supplements. You need about one or two grams of omega-3 (EPA and DHA) daily, but make sure it is mercury purified, if it is derived from fish oil. Do not buy the cheap ones. There are omega supplements available for vegetarians, but some people do not respond well to flax seed oil, and it may increase inflammation. Most people on a Western diet have too much omega-6 and do not need to supplement it. Ideally, you need an equal amount of both omega-3 and omega-6 fats.

Another important fat for your brain are phospholipids. They are needed for brain cell membranes. They also help brain insulation and make up the myelin sheaths around all nerves. The most accessible food for phospholipids is eggs. You can also supplement for them by taking nutritional supplements called Phosphatidyl choline and Phosphatidyl serine. An inexpensive phospholipids supplement is lecithin granules, although it is not to everyone's taste.

Balance Your Blood Sugar

Cravings for substances and a propensity for cross-addiction are associated with unbalanced blood sugar levels. Dr. E. M. Abrahamson, author of *Body, Mind, and Sugar*, believes that hyperinsulinism, which is chronic blood sugar starvation, is a characteristic and contributing factor in alcoholism. Due to alcohol's high caloric content, he believes alcoholics often crave alcohol for its caloric value, and this contributes greatly to relapses. If the alcoholic balances his blood sugar, he will have fewer cravings.[70]

There are three rules to managing your blood sugar levels:

- eat low-GL foods,
- eat protein with carbohydrates, and
- graze, don't gorge—eat little and often.

Glycemic load (GL) is a measure of what a food does to your blood sugar level. Foods with high GL—like sugars and starches—are quickly broken down and absorbed into your bloodstream, and in large amounts will make your blood sugar levels soar. This creates abnormally high peaks and troughs in your blood sugar levels. On the other hand, foods with low GL, like complex carbohydrates (whole grains, vegetables, beans, and lentils), take longer to digest and consequently do not raise your blood sugar levels significantly. Low GL foods are used for energy and not stored; they produce even blood sugar levels and do not cause changes in your behavior, mood, and energy levels. It is beyond the scope of this book to provide lists of different foods and their associated GL levels, but the latter are readily available in many books and on the internet. Another big culprit that wreaks havoc on blood sugar levels is stimulants, like coffee. All forms of stimulants are highly disruptive to blood sugar levels, including energy drinks, chocolates, and fizzy drinks.

When you include fiber and protein with any meal, it slows down the release of carbohydrates, resulting in more stable blood sugar levels. Protein rich foods combined with high-fiber carbohydrates is a good rule of thumb. A simple way to visualize your meals is in quarters. One quarter of your plate protein, another quarter carbohydrates, and the other half vegetables and/or salad. Furthermore, you want to spread out your meals throughout the day. The aim is to keep your blood sugar level stable by eating the right GL foods, so that you don't starve yourself at certain times of the day. It is really important to have a good low GL breakfast—this is when your blood sugar is the lowest—and by breakfast, I do not mean a cup of coffee and a cigarette. To keep blood sugar levels even, it is recommended to have three main meals and a mid-morning and mid-afternoon snack.

A Good Night's Sleep

Having adequate sleep is as important to our well-being as healthy eating and taking supplements. It is no mystery that sleep deprivation leads to poor mental and physical health. Insufficient sleep leads to a significant reduction in certain neurotransmitters, which causes abstinence symptoms and cravings. Addicts in recovery often have poor sleep hygiene and many have sleep problems, especially those who were addicted to "downers." A situation that often leads to poor sleeping habits involves addicts in recovery going to meetings at night and then going for a cup of coffee afterwards. Obviously the coffee can lead to a night of sleeplessness, which can translate into a low mood and cravings the next day.

If you suffer from insomnia, then melatonin is a safe and non-addictive supplement that promotes healthy sleeping patterns. It is suggested that you take between one to three grams half an hour before bedtime. Melatonin is a naturally occurring neurotransmitter produced by the pineal gland that regulates your sleep-wake cycle. Furthermore, taking a calcium and magnesium supplement before bedtime has a relaxing effect. Other sleep hygiene suggestions to improve sleeping habits are keeping the same sleeping hours, avoiding TV or video games before bedtime, keeping your room dark, avoiding caffeine at night, and wearing comfortable bedclothes. Deep breathing exercises, or using a handheld biofeedback device that helps you regulate your breathing to activate the body's relaxation response, may also be helpful. Another practice that helps with sleep problems is using brainwave entrainment CDs that guide your brain into slower frequencies at bedtime. There are many of these CDs available commercially, and this is particularly helpful for people with overactive minds. We will discuss brainwave entrainment in more detail in later chapters.

Exercise

According to Ken Wilber and many other scholars, we have not just one body but three: a gross body, a causal body, and a subtle body. The first, our physical or gross body, is our observable flesh and bones. The gross body is exercised by cardiovascular exercise, like jogging or swimming, and strength training, like weight lifting. The second is our energy or subtle body, which is composed of various energies; the subtle body is exercised by activities like tai chi and yoga. Third is our causal body of "infinite stillness." We get in touch with this body through the practice of meditation. Integral theorists believe that in order to be optimally healthy, we need to exercise all three bodies.

I will discuss the gross and subtle body practices in this chapter and the causal body practices in the chapter on the spiritual recovery dimension. Just a gentle reminder: our aim is not to be at an Olympic standard of physical prowess, but to attain at least a moderately healthy level of fitness. Of course you can take exercise more seriously, but a healthy recovery lifestyle merely suggests reasonable levels of physical health.

Gross Body Practices

It should not be news to you that physical exercise is good for you—this is stating the obvious. New research is continually adding to the existing body of evidence that exercise profoundly affects our health, mood, cognitive, and overall well-being. I believe that for recovering addicts, physical exercise is essential and therefore a central part of an Integrated Recovery Lifestyle. As discussed above, one aspect of the physical manifestation of addiction is an imbalance of neurotransmitters. Exercise has long been known to increase certain mood-enhancing chemicals like endorphins and, for this reason, many psychiatrists and mental health professionals are recommending to their clients, especially those with depression, to exercise. Exercise reduces the release of adrenal stress hormones, increases the supply of blood and oxygen to the brain, and stimulates the release of powerful mood-altering endorphins.

Apart from the physical benefits, exercise helps put you in touch with your body. This is particularly relevant since most addicts are "stuck in their heads" and are disassociated from their bodies and consequently their feelings. Exercise helps your capacity to be mindful and increases emotional intelligence, since we cannot be mindful and in touch with our feelings when we are disconnected from our bodies. Furthermore, exercise has existential value by providing new hobbies, meaning, and spiritual value—just think of jogging on a beach at sunset in a beautiful environment. Exercise also has a social benefit when you engage in a team sport, work out in a gym with your buddy, or go on a surfing weekend with friends. In short, the benefits of exercise are felt in all six recovery dimensions.

There are many ways to get a good cardiovascular workout, and whatever works for you is fine. Swimming, cycling, jogging, martial arts, power walking, surfing, hiking in the mountains, and dancing all work, as long as you build up a sweat and get your heart rate up. I always recommend jogging due to its inexpensive and easily accessible nature. Another form of exercise that I've seen transform addicts' lives is surfing. Just getting into the sea is really beneficial for those in recovery, because it takes you out of your head and relieves you of negative feelings and cravings, while also promoting the release of "feel good" neurotransmitters. For it to have a significant effect, it is normally recommended that you exercise at least three times a week for half an hour at a time. A feature of physical exercise that is of great benefit to recovering addicts, especially in early recovery, is that the results are tangible; you start to feel better quickly, and the results are visible relatively soon. Within weeks, you look and feel better—observable proof that your life in recovery is getting better. Emotional and spiritual progress are often more difficult to notice in oneself.

Another very beneficial form of physical exercise that is highly recommended by many is strength training. Strength training is usually associated with going to the gym. Its many benefits include the release of endorphins, dopamine, epinephrine, and norepinephrine. It also stimulates the production of Brain-Derived Neurotropic Factor (BDNF) as well as Nerve Growth Factor (NGF). All of these help to reduce stress and abate abstinence symptoms. I highly recommend a technique called Focus Intensity Training® (FIT) devised by Shawn Phillips.[71] The amazing thing about this state-of-the-art approach to strength training is that it "makes conscious, coordinated use of the gross, subtle, and causal bodies."[72]

Subtle Body Practices

Energy balancing, or subtle body practices, originated in the medical systems of the Far East, where it has been in use for thousands of years. This system assumes that, apart from our gross bodies, we have a non-physical or subtle energy that permeates and circulates throughout our bodies. This subtle energy has been called different names in various medical traditions—in Indian medicine it's knows as "prana," in Chinese medicine as "chi," in Japanese healing traditions as "ki," and in modern Western culture we describe it as "life force" or "vital energy"—but all of these terms essentially refer to the same phenomenon. From a subtle body perspective, disease is due to various kinds of blockages in the flow of "chi" or vital energy. By practicing energy balancing disciplines like yoga or tai chi, you can release these blocks and restore the natural flow of vital energy. The same is true for subtle body therapies like acupuncture. I believe a "missing link" in our understanding of addiction and recovery is the effect drugs have on our subtle bodies and providing ways of rectifying this damage. There are theories about this topic, but I think they are over-simplified. Recent discoveries in neuroscience show us the damage addiction does to our paleomammalian limbic system. The limbic system correlates to a certain aspect of our subtle body, specifically the emotional energy field. It stands to reason that if our limbic system is damaged, there is correlated damage in our emotional energy field.

There are many subtle body practices—like yoga or tai chi—that heal blockages and strengthen your energy body. Yoga was developed by the Indian philosopher Pantanjali in the second century B.C. The practice of yoga is about unifying body, mind, and spirit, and the word yoga means to "yoke," or unify. Yoga helps with flexibility, relaxation, and increases fitness. Moreover, yoga helps to balance your body energy and promotes the flow of vital energy. When starting with yoga, it is advisable to find a knowledgeable teacher or to join a yoga school. These are easily found in most cities.

Tai chi is an ancient form of movement and exercise that was devised in 13th century China by a Taoist monk. It is often described as a moving meditation. Tai chi consists of a series of movements that strengthen and ground the body while promoting the flow of vital energy or "chi" by helping to release it. Tai chi promotes the unification of body and mind. Like yoga, tai chi is best done with the guidance of a teacher, because the movements are difficult to teach or illustrate via other media.

Physiologically Oriented Therapies

In addition to the practices discussed above, there are also many therapies available that are good for your physical and neurological well-being. If you have used substances for a long time, and even if you don't have any physical problems, it is of benefit to go for therapies that develop a healthy body. I am aware that therapies cost money, and many addicts cannot afford this luxury in early recovery. It is not essential that you go for any of these therapies unless you have a physical condition that needs attention, but they remain an option and are a good investment if you are in the fortunate position to afford them. Many addiction treatment centers have these complementary therapies available as part of an integrative protocol. Many "body" therapies are available, and I will list some commonly used in the context of addiction treatment.

- **Acupuncture**: A Chinese medicine practice where needles are used to decrease or increase the flow of energy along the body's "meridians." A very popular form of acupuncture in treatment environments is auricular therapy—a method of healing that applies stimulation to different acupuncture points on the surface of the ear.

- **Chiropractic:** A chiropractic doctor relieves pain and certain physical problems by manipulation to correct problems in joints, muscles, and spine. Moreover, manipulating the spine will improve energy flow in the body.

- **Kinesiology:** This is a method of maintaining health by ensuring that all muscles are functioning properly. This form of therapy is particularly helpful for uncovering and treating food allergies.

- **Massage:** There are many types of massage therapy available. Massage is particularly helpful in relieving stress that accumulates in the body, and also beneficial for helping the body detox by promoting lymph activity.

- **Reflexology:** An ancient technique of diagnosis and treatment, in which certain areas of the body, particularly the feet, are massaged to alleviate symptoms in the body.

- **Nutrition therapy:** I have already discussed the value of nutrition in the context of recovery. It can be very beneficial to consult a clinical nutritionist knowledgeable about addiction and its effects on the body. If you can only afford one adjunct physical therapy, I recommend nutrition therapy as a priority.

- **Neurofeedback and biofeedback training:** These fall under both the physical and mental/emotional categories. The reason I add neurofeedback (also called neurotherapy) in this section is because it works directly on brain metabolism and physiology. I will add an extra section on this therapy, as I believe it shows great potential in the treatment of addictions.

Neurofeedback

Neurofeedback can be described as a comprehensive training system that promotes growth and metabolic change at the cellular level of the brain. Neurofeedback "trains" an individual's brain to achieve a predetermined goal, while receiving auditory and visual feedback from a specially designed computer program. Research conclusively shows that certain types of abnormal brain functioning can be corrected by learning to condition the brain's electrical activity. Visual/audio electroencephalogram (EEG) feedback is used, by the patient, to learn to increase or decrease the power and/or percentage of selected brainwave frequencies.

Neurofeedback involves recording brain waves, using special electrodes placed on the scalp at specific sites, while displaying the brain's electrical activity on a monitor. As the client learns to alter their own mental state, they increase or decrease the power and/or percentage of selected brainwave frequencies, which are then fed back to him/her through visual and/or audio data. The client attempts to alter their brainwave patterns to achieve a pre-defined goal set up by a neurotherapist.

Biofeedback trains you to develop greater control over your body, and in the case of neurofeedback, your brain. Self-regulation is a training method that engenders long-term positive change. Yoga, meditation, and martial arts—already practiced for centuries—are other ways of gaining control over brain states.

Neurofeedback is based on two principles:

1) that electrical activity in the brain reflects mental states, and

2) that these states can be trained.

Neurofeedback helps your brain to function optimally and is successfully applied to individuals with ADHD, sleep disorders, addictions, autism, and to enhance performance. One of the many benefits of neurofeedback is that it is non-invasive and has no negative side effects—unlike many of the psychiatric drugs that are used to treat the above conditions. Neurofeedback training is shown to be as effective as Ritalin or other stimulant medications in treating ADHD. While in treatment for the harmful effects of mood-altering and addictive substances, addicts are often readily prescribed Ritalin, an amphetamine-like, mood-altering, and addictive stimulant. I've always thought this approach to border on the absurd. Just think about it. Sure, Ritalin does work for ADD, but I should add that heroin also works for pulmonary infections. Effectiveness does not always justify the side effects and potential dangers. I am not saying that addicts cannot take Ritalin, but it should be the last option. A significant percentage of alcoholics and addicts do have ADD or ADHD, and a non-invasive, drug-free treatment that works is obviously of great benefit to the addiction treatment milieu. If you have ADD or ADHD, I strongly recommend neurofeedback training. I have personally witnessed amazing results with this therapy for addicts with ADD/ADHD.

Neurofeedback training has also been shown to be very promising in the treatment of addictions. Eugene Peniston, a pioneer in the treatment of addiction using neurofeedback, has consistently shown remarkable results.[73] He created the Peniston Protocol, a procedure using Neurofeedback training specifically designed to treat those with substance dependence. Other researchers have achieved similar success rates.[74]

Earlier in this chapter, I mentioned that, from one perspective, addiction can be seen as an attempt to rectify neurotransmitter imbalance in the brain. Researchers like Kenneth Blum, developer of the Reward Deficiency Syndrome theory, postulate that the success of neurofeedback training may be due to it triggering a "neurological-normalizing shift" that rectifies neurotransmitter imbalance. Consequently, as Peniston and numerous other researchers have shown, the normalization of alpha and theta EEG rhythms via neurotherapy produces the same normalization of brain chemistry that is produced by either alcohol ingestion or the external manipulation of the excitatory and inhibitory processes that control essential neurochemicals. In other words, the increased feelings of reward and internal well-being that occur from alcohol ingestion or other external influences of brain neurochemistry are also produced by the normalization of alpha and theta rhythms via neurotherapy. Thus, the complex interrelationships among these variables appear to be both at the root of and the cure for severe alcohol cravings and uncontrollable alcohol ingestion.

Some academics and researchers criticize conventional addiction treatment for ignoring the more complex, underlying physiological problems of addiction. They state that without improving a recovering addict's neurophysiology, treatment is often fruitless or incomplete.[75] I believe one of the significant factors that contribute to the high relapse rate after treatment is that most treatment models do not address and rectify the neurological imbalances caused by, and resulting, from addiction. Most agree that addiction is a brain disease but few incorporate modalities that directly target physiological healing of the brain in their treatment protocol. Therapies like neurofeedback training that target physiological healing in the brain are needed for treatment programs to be truly comprehensive and effective. The combination of neurofeedback training and a well-designed nutritional supplement protocol (applied in conjunction with existing evidence-based treatment models) is one of the most exciting new elements of addiction treatment and, when deployed, will significantly increase the success rate of treatment centers.

Designing the Physical Recovery Dimension of your IRP

After all of this information about the many aspects of the physical recovery dimension, you might feel a bit overwhelmed in designing the physical recovery dimension of your Integrated Recovery Program. Don't worry, it seems more complicated than it really is. Moreover, all of this information will not be relevant to you at all times in your recovery. The components that you need to ensure that you remain stable and relatively healthy are:

- Diet
- Supplements
- Medication (if any)
- Sleep
- Exercise
- Physical therapies (optional)

See, not that complicated. Just ensure that your diet is reasonably healthy, you are getting enough sleep and exercise, take some supplements, and apply adjunct physical therapies when appropriate and affordable. In short, ensure that your physical condition is at an acceptable standard and that there are no deficiencies that can compromise your new lifestyle.

The following suggestions and exercises will assist in designing and choosing the appropriate practices that will ensure that your physical recovery dimension is functioning adequately for your current stage of recovery.

1. Diet: Make some notes about your diet considering the information in this chapter. Aspects to look for are: regularity of meals, organic or not, amount, quality, junk food, vegetables, fruit, amount and regularity of water, coffee, and energy drinks. After writing down the facts of your dietary habits it should become evident which areas are fine and which need to be improved. The best option is to see a nutritionist if you can afford it.

2. Supplements: Make notes about all the supplements you are currently taking. Make notes about the supplements you intend on taking, based either on the information in this chapter or on information received from a nutritionist or through additional reading. Identify supplements that are lacking in your current regime. See if you can afford those on your list. If finances are an issue, buy supplements that are the most important for you now. Remember, do NOT take supplements if you are on medication without consulting the appropriate parties.

3. Medication: If you are on medication, write down what you take and how often. Are you happy with your current medication? Are you sticking to your

appointments with your psychiatrist? Are you taking your medication as prescribed? Do you want to stop your medication? Remember ALWAYS seek professional help when terminating medication.

4. Sleep: Make notes about your sleeping habits. If you have a problem in this regard, write down your plans to improve your sleep cycle.

5. Exercise: Make notes about your exercise routine. If you feel that it is inadequate, write up your ideal routine and explore its practical possibilities. Write additional notes if you feel you might be over exercising or creating any injuries or damage. Consider if you need to join a group or organization or get a personal trainer.

6. Physical therapies: Make notes regarding any presenting physical problems you may have. Consider the option of physical therapy for the problem(s). Explore the financial investment and decide on the appropriateness of your plan. If there are no presenting physical problems but you would like to increase your general physical well-being, explore practices that are appropriate and affordable for you currently.

7. Make notes on any thoughts or feelings regarding your physical self or your physical practices. Are you procrastinating? Do you have unrealistic expectations of your physical routine? Are you focusing too much attention on exercise and physical well-being at the expense of other aspects of your Integrated Recovery Lifestyle? Are you using exercise as a way to escape

feelings of shame and low self-worth? Add any additional thoughts and feelings.

8. Finally, make notes about issues you need to discuss with your therapist, sponsor, or coach. Part of an Integrated Recovery Lifestyle is to live "in consultation." Therefore, make sure you discuss any major plans or changes in your physical recovery dimension with people in your support system, especially when in early recovery. You don't have to phone your sponsor every time you go jogging, but if you decide on a new therapy or practice, first check with those in your support system.

CHAPTER 4
THE INTELLECTUAL RECOVERY DIMENSION

*In Mind Nature at last emerges from the
deep sleep of its far-off beginnings, becomes
awake, aware and conscious, begins to know
herself, and consciously, instead of blindly and
unconsciously, to reach out towards freedom,
towards welfare, and towards the goal
of the ultimate Good.*
~ Jan Smuts

"Know thyself," said the Delphic motto. In 12-step culture, knowing and thinking take on a paradoxical nature. On one hand, recovering addicts are advised, as in the Delphic motto, to "know themselves" through introspective practices like journaling and doing step work, but on the other hand they are told, "Ask how not why," "Remember your best thinking got you here," "Your head is a dangerous neighborhood, and you should not go in there alone," and so forth. Addicts are warned of the dangers of thinking and knowing. For the casual observer, this might appear to be contradictory. Because of these warnings, recovery is often erroneously viewed as an anti-intellectual approach. This view is simply inaccurate. What the collective wisdom of the 12-step fellowships warns against are merely the limitations of logical thought—but it does not deny the central value of thinking and cognitive insight for sustainable recovery.

A similar view is shared in Zen Buddhism, where the novice is warned against the dangers that conceptual thought holds for him in his quest for realization of the true nature of things— reality cannot truly be grasped through concepts. In the same way, recovery cannot be grasped through thinking alone—as in Zen, you must "taste" recovery to truly know it. The philosopher Immanuel Kant echoes the above when he "argued that neither our intellectual understanding nor our rational mind alone could lead us to any knowledge of what things are in themselves or what we are in ourselves, since our understanding could not penetrate beyond the realms and limits of our possible experience."[76] The paradoxical suggestions in the 12-step fellowships point to this limitation of logic. They suggest that you must think but not assume that you can solve the problem of your addiction and life by thinking alone—it has its limitations. This is because the experienced recovering addict knows that a characteristic of addiction is to believe in the certainty of and empirical validity of our thoughts—and the only way to "get" or truly taste recovery is to suspend our judgments about ourselves and the world and to move into the realm of "not-knowing." Zen scholar Steve Hagen states: "By our very attempt to grasp an explanation, we leave things out. In just such a manner, to take any frozen view is to leave out a piece of Reality. What we repeatedly fail to notice is that there is never a static object to observe—nor, for that matter, a static, clearly-defined observer."[77]

From an existential perspective, the addict usually has a serious problem with accepting his limits of being and with control. This self-proclaimed control translates into the deeply held certainty of his beliefs. Furthermore, due to the developmentally regressive nature of addiction, the addict's certainty will consequently become more and more partial and insane—but his desperate need to control and cling to his beloved "certainties" remains. The more "wrong" his beliefs, the more certain he becomes. Step One is not just the simple acknowledgment of powerlessness over substances, but an authentic realization and acknowledgment of "not-knowing." I often say to neophytes in recovery, the only thing you must know for certain is how to use a phone. This enables you to "live in consultation" by asking questions—and if you phone enough people, you will eventually get the answers you need. The simple act of phoning a sponsor or reaching out to another addict is a profound statement of existential limitation. It is only by knowing our limitations that we can start to develop a more authentic view of ourselves, the world, and our place in it.

There is a movement in popular self-help culture to actualize our "infinite potential" and so forth, but if this is not firmly grounded in the realization of our limitations and "insignificance" in the relative sense, it merely flatters our "false ego," and we become too big for our "Cosmic shoes." I believe Wilber refers to this condition as "Boomeritis." This is an integral part of addiction—an inflated false ego to protect the shame we feel about ourselves—and is often further perpetuated by a sense of perceived isolation and insignificance. Recovery is the exact role reversal of this pathology. AA and NA's warning against the limitations of rational knowledge does not mean that you don't or did not know anything, but rather that what you know is only a piece of the bigger picture. Consequently, recovery requires a certain degree of faith—not blind faith, but a leap of faith into the unknown by trusting those who leapt before us. Although many addicts have a problem with the concept of faith and trust in early recovery, they certainly did not have a problem with faith in trying out different drugs—I seldom saw heroin addicts debate the ontological nature, origin, and chemical structure of their bag of heroin before they shot it up. So, if in recovery you have a problem with this "faith" thing, just use some of the "open-mindedness" you displayed in relation to your drugs and you will be just fine.

This leap of faith and suspension of understanding has pragmatic value in recovery. If the neophyte in recovery must wait until s/he understands all the elements of the program, s/he may die. It is for this reason that many addicts need to "hit bottom," to reach existential despair—which wears down their rational mind with its insistence on understanding before doing—before many are ready to just do what is required. As it says in the *Big Book* of AA, "Alcohol was a great persuader. It finally beat us into a state of reasonableness."[78] It is when we surrender to our limited understanding of ourselves and the world, when we become receptive and begin to do—this is when recovery begins. This holds true for the neophyte and the old timer. Recovery is characterized by openness, receptiveness, and fluidity, whereas addiction is characterized by closed-mindedness and rigid certainty. For this reason, I have always seen a great deal of resemblance between 12-step and Taoist philosophy. Lao Tzu, the ancient Taoist philosopher, says:

> It is better to leave a vessel unfilled, than to attempt to carry it when it is full... The thirty spokes unite in one nave; but it is on the empty space, that the use of the wheel depends. Clay is fashioned into vessels; but it is on their empty hollowness, that their use depends. The door and windows are cut out to form an apartment; but it is on the empty space, that its use depends. Therefore, what has a positive existence serves for profitable adaption, and what has not that for actual usefulness.[79]

Now that we know what we don't know—let's look at what we can and should know.

Recovery Map

Everyone would agree that when you are traveling in unknown territory, you need an accurate map. In many ways, the Integrated Recovery approach provides just such a map for the recovery "territory." Obviously, recovery is a fluid and often mercurial process, as with any transformational path, but there are nonetheless certain familiar touchstones and markers along the way. For your recovery lifestyle to be effective, you need a certain amount of knowledge and intellectual understanding of what is happening and what you should be doing, as well as a healthy dose of curiosity about how and why this whole thing works. In short, we need to practice our cognitive or intellectual aspect of our Integrated Recovery Lifestyle. This area of practice is referred to as the intellectual recovery dimension of your Integrated Recovery Program.

The intellectual dimension is not new to 12-step culture; historically a lot of emphasis is placed on study and written work. Working the steps often refers to, among other things, doing written work with your sponsor or therapist. Twelve-step fellowships know we need a certain amount of intellectual insight into ourselves, others, and the world. As said before, this is tempered by the spiritual principle of humility in accepting the limitations of our intellect and with a "certainty" of its partiality. What makes the Integrated Recovery approach unique is that it reframes the 12-step culture from an integrally informed perspective and augments it with an understanding of mindfulness, existentialism and positive psychology. This is in keeping with the spirit of Integral Theory, which recognizes the partial truth of most points of view, keeping what is best in them, but also adding what is lacking.

In this chapter, we look at practices and therapies that promote cognitive understanding of our Integrated Recovery Lifestyle. The inclusion of Integral Theory, mindfulness, existentialism, and positive psychology has one particular benefit for recovering addicts—it breaks the dichotomy between addict and non-addict. As recovering addicts, we see that our journey is not very different from those pursuing other paths of self-discovery. I believe this integrates addicts into a larger sangha or world community of like-minded seekers, while maintaining a sense of belonging to their particular fellowships. This is especially significant when we enter a worldcentric stage of development. In Integral circles, this is often referred to as "dual-citizenship." In this chapter, we will also look at the significance of working the Twelve Steps in a written format. I will explore the value of literature and workshops and provide a list of suggested reading.

Working the Steps

As indicated before, the Integrated Recovery approach is to a great extent informed by the 12-step program. When "working" each of these steps, one is normally required to do so in the form of written work, which is then processed with a sponsor or therapist. You can find "step work questions" in most conference-approved literature of the respective fellowships. For instance, in NA they have the *Step Working Guide*. Apart from fellowship literature, there are many other step working guides available, such as *A Gentle Path Though the Twelve Steps* by Patrick Carnes. All of these workbooks are designed to provide, among other things, cognitive insight into the steps and ultimately into ourselves. Doing written step work is psychoactive. I have yet to come across a modality that creates such rapid healing and transformation as the written 12-step work in the 12-step program. Written work is an essential and indispensable aspect of working a 12-step program.

John Bradshaw, in his bestselling book *Healing the Shame that Binds You,* provides a helpful viewpoint of the Twelve Steps from a perspective of how it helps transform toxic shame. Bradshaw believes that what ultimately fuels addiction is toxic shame. Bradshaw adheres to a more traditional interpretation of the steps and its language. For individuals like myself, who have an atheistic worldview, the "religious undertones" must be reframed in a way that makes it digestible. The Twelve Steps is often described as a spiritual program; while this may be true for some, I believe the essence of it is existential, as it directs us to explore what we believe gives our lives meaning. This might be a spiritual understanding for some, but certainly not essential. The essential and curative component is finding meaning in our lives. My personal view is that the use of the words "God" and "Higher Power" is unnecessary and counterproductive in our contemporary society, as many people are put off by these concepts. One often hears members say, "when we use the word God, we don't really mean God." Perhaps in the future, 12-step fellowships will replace these archaic terms. Obviously, if someone has a religious or spiritual worldview that he/she finds meaningful, it should be accommodated within the 12-step framework.

Step One of NA states, "We admitted that we were powerless over our addiction, that our lives had become unmanageable." Bradshaw believes this step makes apparent the most powerful aspect of any shame syndrome and addiction—"its functional autonomy." He quotes an old adage about alcohol that illustrates this point:

> Man takes a drink.
> Drink takes a drink.
> Drink takes a man.[80]

Step One is about coming out of hiding and admitting the power that our addiction has over us. As we surrender to this reality of our addiction, we are also accepted by a loving fellowship—the interpersonal bridge begins to repair as we expose our shame to others.

Step Two states, "We came to believe that a Power greater than ourselves could restore us to sanity." In this step, we reach out to something greater than ourselves; it is the logical conclusion of Step One.

In Step Three, which states: "We made a decision to turn our will and our lives over to the care of God as we understood Him," there is conscious mention of God, but the fellowships leave it up to their members to devise their own conception of a Higher Power. This is a very pluralistic perspective, as it gives anybody, regardless of their spiritual or existential development and understanding, an opportunity to access and contemplate what they find meaningful. Steps Two and Three curtail one's own God-playing.

"Shame-based people also do not believe *they have the right to depend on anyone*. This is a consequence of the violated dependency needs that were ruptured through the abandonment trauma. To turns one's will and life over to God is to restore a right relationship of dependence. To go to meetings and trust other people is to risk depending again."[81] This restores a sense of healthy shame; we are human—fallible, and dependent. Wilber also points out that we need healthy shame to move from egocentric to ethnocentric levels of development. Bradshaw says that the first three steps "restore the proper relationship between ourselves and the source of life."[82] Additionally, from an existential perspective, "we re-join the human race; we accept our need for community and the essential limitations of our human reality."[83]

Step Four states: "We made a searching and fearless moral inventory of ourselves." Here we begin restoring our relationship with others. We learn that we are okay and that fortunately, our former wrongdoings can be remedied. In this step, we continue the process of turning toxic shame into healthy shame.

In Step Five, which states: "We admitted to God, to ourselves, and to another human being the exact nature of our wrongs," we come out of hiding. We expose our shame to another person, but find that we are accepted, fundamentally okay, and that our character defects are changeable.

Step Six states, "We were entirely ready to have God remove all these defects of character." When asking for the removal of character defects, we do so under the presumption that we are worthy and allow ourselves to be dependent in a healthy way.

In Step Seven, which states: "We humbly asked Him to remove our shortcomings," we are restored to healthy shame. We admit our faults but also our capacity to change and grow.

Steps Eight and Nine respectively state that; "We made a list of all persons we have harmed and became willing to make amends to them all," and "We made direct amends to such people wherever possible, except when to do so would injure them or others." In these steps we restore our relationship with others. Shame-based people feel they cannot be intimate, because when they are intimate, they have to expose their real selves.

Steps Ten, Eleven, and Twelve help to maintain the restored relationships. Step Ten states, "We continued to take personal inventory and when we were wrong promptly admitted it." Bradshaw says Step Ten "is the maintenance relationship step with ourselves. It keeps us in touch with our healthy shame, the emotion that tells us we can and will make mistakes. By continually being in touch with our fundamental humanness and our essential limitations, we can accept ourselves. To acknowledge our mistakes is to embrace and express our vulnerability and our finitude. Such a consciousness keeps tabs on our tendency to become grandiose and shameless."[84]

In Step Eleven, which states: "We sought through prayer and meditation to improve our conscious contact with God as we understood Him, praying only for knowledge of His will for us and the power to carry that out," we continue to deepen our bond and mutuality with our "Higher Power" or with whatever we find meaningful in the world.

Step Twelve acknowledges the spiritual awakening that results from working these steps. Step Twelve states: "Having had a spiritual awakening as a result of these steps, we tried to carry this message to addicts and to practice these principles in all our affairs." We are moved to help others "as we model our restored relationships with God, self, our neighbors and the world, we can show others there is a way out. There is hope."[85]

Recovery Literature

The use of literature has traditionally played an essential role in recovery. Nearly everyone's recovery starts by reading something, either a pamphlet or a book. I will not say too much about the value of literature, as I will be "preaching to the choir." The fact that you are still reading this book means you know the value of reading and studying texts. Although the scope of Integrated Recovery is broad, here I will mainly focus on books about personal development. In this section, I provide a list of suggested readings drawn from 12-step-based, mindfulness, existentialism, positive psychology, and Integral Theory texts and books that may be useful to you in designing an Integrated Recovery Program—or just for inspiration. This list is not exhaustive, but merely a selection of literature that provides intelligent and practical insight in its respective fields. You need not read all of these books in order to work your program or to be familiar with Integrated Recovery Theory. This suggested list is merely for those who are interested in further study in a particular area.

Twelve Steps and Recovery:

- ❖ Alcoholics Anonymous—AA World Services, Inc. (Alcoholism)
- ❖ Narcotics Anonymous—NA World Services, Inc. (Drug Addiction)
- ❖ It Works, How and Why—NA World Services, Inc. (Drug Addiction)
- ❖ The Narcotic Anonymous Step Working Guides—NA World Services, Inc. (Drug Addiction)
- ❖ Out of the Shadows—Patrick Carnes (Sex Addiction)
- ❖ Facing the Shadow—Patrick Carnes (Sex Addiction)
- ❖ Recovery Zone Volume 1—Patrick Carnes (General Recovery)
- ❖ Is it Love or is it Addiction—Brenda Schaeffer (Love Addiction)
- ❖ Facing Love Addiction—Pia Melody (Love Addiction)
- ❖ Open Hearts—Patrick Carnes et al. (Relationship Recovery)
- ❖ Co-Dependence—Charles Whitfield (Co-Dependency)
- ❖ Healing the Shame that Binds You—John Bradshaw (General Recovery)
- ❖ Home Coming—John Bradshaw (Adult Child and General Recovery)
- ❖ Trauma and Addiction—Tian Dayton (General Recovery)

Positive Psychology:

- ❖ Authentic Happiness—Martin Seligman
- ❖ Flourish—Martin Seligman

Mindfulness:

- ❖ Wherever You Go There You Are—Jon Kabat-Zinn
- ❖ Full Catastrophy Living—Jon Kabat-Zinn
- ❖ Coming to Our Senses—Jon Kabat-Zinn
- ❖ The Miracle of Mindfulness—Thich Nhat Hanh
- ❖ Mindful Recovery—Thomas & Beverly Bien
- ❖ Eating Mindfully—Susan Albers

Existentialism:

- ❖ Thus Spoke Zarathustra—Friedrich Nietzsche
- ❖ The Outsider—Colin Wilson
- ❖ Steppenwolf—Hermann Hesse
- ❖ Narziss and Goldmund—Herman Hesse
- ❖ The Myth of Sisyphus—Albert Camus
- ❖ Existentialism—John Macquarrie
- ❖ Man's Search for Meaning—Viktor Frankl

Integral Theory:

- ❖ A Brief History of Everything—Ken Wilber
- ❖ Integral Psychology—Ken Wilber
- ❖ Integral Spirituality—Ken Wilber
- ❖ Integral Life Practice—Ken Wilber et al.

- ❖ Integral Recovery—John Dupuy
- ❖ A Guide to Integral Psychotherapy—Mark Forman
- ❖ Inside Out/Outside In—Ingersoll & Zeitler

Additional Reading:

- ❖ Strength for Life—Shawn Philips
- ❖ The Spirituality of Imperfection—Ernest Kurtz and Katherine Ketcham
- ❖ Mind-Body Workbook for PTSD—Stanley Block
- ❖ Coming to Your Senses—Stanley Block
- ❖ The Voice Dialogue Manual—Hal and Sidra Stone
- ❖ The Joy Beyond Craving—Joni Rose
- ❖ Drugs, Addiction, and Initiation—Luigi Zoja
- ❖ A New Earth—Eckhart Tolle
- ❖ The Sun Rises in the Evening—Gary Nixon
- ❖ How to be an Adult in Relationships—David Richo
- ❖ Craving for Ecstasy and Natural Highs—Harvey Milkman and Stanley Sunderwirth
- ❖ The Globalization of Addiction—Bruce Alexander
- ❖ Witness to the Fire—Linda Leonard
- ❖ Pathways—William White

Designing the Intellectual Recovery Dimension of Your IRP

In designing the intellectual recovery dimension of your Integrated Recovery Program, there are a couple of aspects you need to consider to ensure adequate cognitive insight into your Integrated Recovery Lifestyle. They are:

- Twelve-step written work
- Literature
- Workshops, seminars, and lectures (optional)

In a nutshell, ensure that you are doing 12-step written work and reading enough literature to provide you with intellectual insight into your addiction and recovery. Also, attend lectures and workshops when you have the opportunity. Healthy debate and discussion is a further practice. One of the joys of my recovery were the times when I had "profound" late night debates about recovery with fellow recovering addicts. Healthy debate stimulates different perspectives and/or strengthens your existing perspective—either way, it is positive. I must add that intellectual insight is only truly useful when it translates into change, and more often than not, new insight must be practiced for it to be sustained. A lot of personal development literature can actually be detrimental if not practiced. It is for this reason that certain traditions like Zen warn of the dangers of knowledge without a true "flesh and bones" understanding of that knowledge. Addiction is characterized by being too "top heavy"—so do not add to the problem by adding more to your head without changing your heart and behavior.

The following suggestions and exercises will help you design and choose the appropriate practices to ensure that your intellectual recovery dimension is functioning adequately.

1. Twelve-step written work: Make notes about the step work you are currently working on. If procrastinating, explore the reasons why you are not as productive as you would like to be. Remember, it is normal to resist step work, but it is useful to have insight into

the reason(s) why. And write down a plan of action to overcome these stumbling blocks.

2. Literature: Write down what literature you are currently reading as well as what books you would like to read in the near future. Explore the possibilities of you over-investing or under-investing in literature. Moreover, are you following the suggestions in what you are reading, or is this merely remaining an intellectual pursuit.

3. Are you attending any lectures or workshops? What areas of your Integrated Recovery Lifestyle do you want to learn more about? What is stopping you from learning more? Are there any ways you can overcome these difficulties?

4. Are you processing the written work with your sponsor or therapist? Remember, an important component of doing step work is to process the written work with somebody else. If you are not working with a sponsor, think of the reasons for this. If your reasons are logistical, are there ways to overcome these obstacles?

5. Write down some general notes regarding your intellectual process since entering recovery. It is often useful to see what progress one has made. Draw a time-line indicating significant intellectual events, books read, as well as insights starting from the day you entered treatment until now.

CHAPTER 5
THE PSYCHOLOGICAL RECOVERY DIMENSION

*The greatest discovery of my generation is
that human beings can alter their lives by
altering their attitudes of mind.*
~ William James

We now realize that feelings are much more important than originally thought. Psychologist Silvan Tompkins believes feelings are the primary biological motivating force of human behavior. He believes "the primary blueprint for cognition, decision, and action is provided by the effect system."[86] For Tomkins, feeling is a mode of thinking and therefore inseparable from decision and action. In his book *Descartes' Error,* neuroscientist Antonio Damasio supports Tompkins' position in pointing out that when we damage the part of our brain that controls feelings, we cannot make decisions. Tompkins goes on to say that "without feeling, nothing matters, and with feeling, anything can matter."[87] Emotional intelligence is therefore essential for effective living. Perls adds, "If emotion is, as I have hypothesized, the basic force that energizes all action, it exists in every life situation. One of the most serious problems of modern man is that he has desensitized himself to all but the most overwhelming kind of emotional response. To the degree that he is no longer capable of feeling sensitively, to that degree he becomes incapable of the freedom of choice that results in a relevant action."[88]

The psychological component of your Integrated Recovery Program refers to all the aspects that relate to your inner psychic-emotional life. Traditionally, this is the realm of psychiatry and psychology. For our purposes, this recovery dimension covers all therapeutic, emotional, and psychological factors relating to an individual. Obviously our intellectual and existential recovery dimensions are interrelated with the psychological dimension, but as mentioned before, this is a pragmatic abstract division. The aim of this part of your Integrated Recovery Program is to work on your emotional intelligence and psychological health, and to uncover shadow material.

Addicts are known to have turbulent and overwhelming inner worlds. Addiction is often referred to as an attempt at "self-medicating" the addict's painful and confusing inner world. According to Edward Khantzian, psychiatrist and object-relations theorist, the reason that addicts have such fragmented inner worlds is that they often have "defects in ego and self capacities which leave such people ill-equipped to regulate and modulate feelings, self-esteem, relationships, and behavior."[89] It is widely believed in reputable treatment centers that emotional intelligence is important for the recovering addict to achieve sustained recovery. Addiction is caused by, and causes, emotional illiteracy.

The Cycle of Addiction and Trauma

For humans to survive when young, they need close, bonded relationships. Psychotherapist, and author of the book *Trauma and Addiction,* Tian Dayton calls these essential relationships "survival bonds." We are designed in such a way that we are rewarded when forming these bonds, because the survival of our species depends on it. When, as infants, we are in close, intimate contact with our mothers, our brains release a "reward chemical" known as beta endorphin, similar to morphine.[90] When these bonds are threatened, we experience terror or rage, and when these bonds are ruptured, we feel as "if our inner and outer worlds are falling apart."[91] When these ruptures occur, infants experience serious trauma. Rupturing of early bonds is the most traumatic, but any subsequent bond dysfunction creates further trauma. These traumatic memories are stored in our minds and bodies (and likely our energy bodies as well) and are collectively referred to as cellular memory. Candace Pert, the famous neuroscientist who discovered the opioid receptor, states that, "Intelligence is located not only in the brain, but in cells that are distributed throughout the body... The memory of trauma is stored by changes at the level of the neuropeptide receptor... This is taking place bodywide."[92]

If we were traumatized as children, we will be left with significant deficits in our psychological development and in our ability to engage in healthy nurturing relationships—making us prone to addiction in later life. "When our basic life needs are not met adequately early in life, we develop an emotional hunger that is never met and is characterized by our seeking to redo the past—to meet our early unmet needs with the wrong people at the wrong time and place."[93] This inner emptiness, loneliness, and pain—coupled with a fear of and deficit in the ability to form intimate relationships—leaves us with few options to meet our needs other than to reach out for something "non-intimate," like substances. When traumatized, our ability to self-regulate is compromised. That is why addicts are often characterized by poor self-regulation skills and poor impulse control. Addiction is often a dysfunctional attempt to self-soothe, and bring some peace to our anxious, empty, and confusing inner worlds. What makes matters worse is that a "traumatized person does not have access to the left hemisphere of the brain which translates experience into language, therefore, they can't make meaning out of what is happening to them or put it into any context. Traumatized people have been known to have trouble tolerating intense emotions without feeling overwhelmed and thus continue to rely on disassociation."[94]

Addicts are known to be out of touch with their emotions. They have difficulty feeling certain emotions as well as naming and tolerating them. Addicts often experience feelings as vague, overpowering sensations over which they perceive they have little control. This lack of inner control is often a frightening experience. In this context, addiction is seen as addicts' dysfunctional attempt to control their out-of-control inner worlds. Our substance of choice becomes our main method of mood management and temporarily restores our inner equilibrium. That is why we often hear addicts say things like, "I never felt normal until I started using drugs," or "I always felt like there was something missing inside and when I took drugs I felt complete." One of the many problems with this method is that it further denies access to our internal world, which we must access in order to resolve our trauma. "While trauma victims gain the temporary relief they are seeking [by self-medicating], they do so at the expense of self-knowledge and the potential for self-mastery."[95] I will quote Flores at length as he superbly describes the cause and progress of addiction from a psychodynamic perspective.

> Addiction... is viewed as a misguided attempt at self-repair. Because of unmet developmental needs, certain individuals will be left with an injured, enfeebled, uncohesive, or fragmented self. Such individuals often look good on the outside, but are empty and feel incomplete on the inside. They are unable to regulate affect and in many cases are even unable to identify what it is that they feel. Unable to draw on their own internal resources because there are not any, they remain in constant need (object hunger) of having those self-regulating resources met externally—out there. Since painful, rejecting, and shaming relationships are the cause of their deficits in self, they cannot turn to others to get what they need or have never received. Deprivation of needs and object hunger leaves them with unrealistic and intolerable affects that are not only disturbing to others, but shameful to themselves. Consequently, alcohol, drugs, and other external sources of gratification (i.e., food,

sex, work, etc.) take on a regulating function while creating a false sense of autonomy, independence, and denial of need for others... addiction is an attempt at self-help that fails.[96]

What makes matters even worse is that the addictive process becomes autonomous—a phenomenon known as "functional autonomy"—and begins to take on a life of its own. "The withdrawal from authentic emotions and alienation from the self that the drug induces leaves trauma victims helpless before their own internal world, and the "learned helplessness" of the trauma victim is thereby reinforced."[97] Addiction becomes a vicious cycle—the more we medicate our unresolved pain the less able we are to deal with it. Addiction then creates further trauma that also remains unresolved. The result of years of unresolved and repressed feelings and trauma is that many addicts reach a point where mere feelings associated with being "straight" become an unbearable torture. This enlightens us as to why a good self-help book cannot break this vicious cycle. Literally, the addict has lost all volition of his inner world and behavior and now sits in the passenger seat of his dysfunctional "psychic bus."

Breaking the Cycle Through Emotional Literacy[98]

An essential component of recovery is becoming emotionally literate and dealing with unresolved trauma. If this does not happen, our addiction may continually migrate, seeking dysfunctional ways to deal with the unresolved trauma. This is a very common occurrence in 12-step fellowships. One of the most commonly used defenses, when faced with trauma, is to go numb or freeze, therefore we are often not conscious of these areas of disowned pain. Some scholars believe this is why we re-enact our early traumas in adult relationships. It is an attempt to make the unconscious conscious. The re-enactment of trauma is often seen when addicts enter into relationships in early recovery. From this perspective, we see why relationships in early recovery are often disastrous. Addicts in early recovery are by default attracted to somebody who will re-enact the unresolved trauma. When the trauma is re-enacted, they lack the emotional maturity to cope with the resulting emotional turmoil and then often revert to the coping skills they know best—using drugs.

To deal with our unresolved issues and un-metabolized pain, we must become emotionally literate, acquiring the ability to accurately tune in to our internal world and then to act appropriately on the information we've received. We need to put feelings into words so that we can understand these feelings within some form of psychological context. The problem with memories of trauma is that they bypass the cortex and are stored in other parts of the brain such as the basal forebrain and amygdala. Consequently, we do not always have full access to these memories. On the other hand, talking about trauma allows us to name our feelings, and over time allows our memories to be lifted out of a semiconscious state into our consciousness. As a result, we can begin to modulate our emotions and slowly gain mastery of our inner worlds. Tian Dayton identifies four stages of progression in developing emotional literacy:

- **Stage One: Feel the Fullness of the Emotion**
  We need to learn to sit with our feelings. We

cannot begin to understand our inner world if we first do not learn to fully experience it. The first stage is merely to feel our feelings in all of their dimensions.

- **Stage Two: Label It**
  Next we need to name our emotional experiences. Naming or labeling emotions makes us feel better. Scientists have shown that labeling feelings elevates the immune system. Furthermore, labeling and the development of emotional awareness help build emotional resilience, which enables us to handle difficult emotions better in the future.

- **Stage Three: Explore the Meaning and Function Within the Self**
  In this stage, we explore the meaning that feelings and state-experiences have within our inner worlds. Is your behavior in line with your feelings? Are they congruent? Understanding the nature of our inner worlds is a complex process. Moreover, knowing the function that thoughts and feelings have within the self-system requires considerable self-reflection.

- **Stage Four: Choose Whether or Not to Communicate Our Inner State to Another Person**

At the fourth stage we have a choice. We now understand our inner experiences and can choose what to do with this information. To have full emotional literacy, we must have the capacity to share our inner worlds with others. Moreover, we must be able to know with whom it is appropriate to share our experiences and also be able to engage in back-and-forth communication.

Emotional literacy is an acquired skill like playing the guitar; to be emotionally literate, we need to be educated and practice the skill. Addicts are usually profoundly emotionally illiterate—either because it was never taught to them and/or due to years of addiction. Therefore, a pivotal aspect of any recovery process needs to be guidance in and practice of the development of emotional literacy.

The Shadow

The shadow, Carl Jung says, represents everything that an individual refuses to acknowledge about himself, and therefore the shadow is always forcing itself upon him directly or indirectly. The aspects of our traumas and experiences that, for whatever reason, we were unable to integrate and process become unconscious—turn into shadow material. The founder of psychoanalysis Sigmund Freud listed many primary and secondary defenses we use to protect ourselves against overwhelming anxiety—all of which contribute to our shadow. These processes do not only happen when we are young but may continue throughout life, as we continue to disown parts of our personality that do not fit in with our image of ourselves. We may then repress, reject, deny, or project this onto others. Moreover, addiction, by default, creates vast amounts of shadow material— it is commonly known that denial is one of the biggest stumbling blocks for sustainable recovery. Denial can also be understood as the denial of our shadow. The purpose of shadow work is to undo these repressions and bring the shadow material into the light, and finally, to integrate it—which promotes psychological health and clarity.

There are many ways to do shadow work. One of the greatest contributions of Western philosophy/psychology is its contribution to our understanding of the shadow, and the development of many psychotherapeutic techniques. The field of psychotherapy is incredibly diverse and often confusing to practitioners and scholars, because different schools of thought wrestle for dominance and credibility. Many schools of psychotherapy prove themselves right by proving others wrong. This is most unfortunate as it merely causes fragmentation in the discipline. Eclectic and integrative approaches to psychotherapy have gained recent popularity, which has certainly counteracted some of the fragmentation. The emerging field of Integral Psychotherapy is an attempt to integrate and make sense of all these diverse approaches by finding value in all the diverse schools of psychotherapy.

For recovery to be effective and sustainable, we need to engage in shadow work at certain times in our process. Addiction thrives in our shadow, and, if left unprocessed and unchecked, it is most certainly bound to cause relapse and/or cross-addiction. The problem with the shadow is that even though it is unconscious, it requires a great deal of energy to keep it unconscious;

furthermore, it sends negative signals and destructive impulses to our consciousness. The more shadow material we have, the less conscious control we have in our lives; we can be controlled by unconscious impulses like a leaf blowing in the wind. Have you ever heard somebody say, "I promised myself I would never be like my father/mother, but I have become just like him/her?" This is shadow in action. How else could we end up doing things that we consciously want to avoid? Put simply, the shadow often lets you do the things you least want to do.

Working through shadow material gives us conscious control of our lives. This is as important for people in long-term recovery as for those in early recovery. As we develop to higher levels of consciousness in recovery, our shadow material becomes more complex, often more intense, and even more difficult to navigate. It was only after many years clean—and with the naive belief that by then I had worked through my issues—that I was confronted with some very powerful shadow impulses and was plunged into deep confusion and pain. Each level of recovery brings on new possible shadow pathologies. So, just because you have been clean for ten years, have done a couple of Step Fours, and spent two years dealing with adult child issues, does not mean you are "shadowless." As soon as you have kids, or get married, or enter a new stage of personal growth, pathology and "unresolved issues" lurk somewhere. A healthy Integrated Recovery Lifestyle means to be ready to do "shadow work" when nessesary. Don't worry, this does not mean endless therapy, endless morbid self-introspection, and daily emotional excavation work. There are simple methods to keep us psychologically healthy, as well as more intensive methods for if and when the need arises.

Now we will explore several self-help practices that stimulate emotional literacy and health: Steps Four and Ten, the 3-2-1 Shadow Process, the mindfulness of emotion skill used in Dialectic Behavior Therapy (DBT), and Rational Emotive Behavior Therapy (REBT). We can use all of these skills on our own, without a therapist. Following that, I will discuss therapies that deal with shadow and mental health issues.

Steps Four & Ten

We discussed working the steps in the previous chapter, but I think Steps Four and Ten merit special mention here. Step Four is very effective shadow work—one big "clearing of the basement." In this step, "We made a searching and fearless moral inventory of ourselves,"[99] we start owning our character defects and often realize we're not as nice and cool as we thought. Although addicts have low self-esteem and frequently acknowledge how badly they have screwed up, they still may, due to narcissistic defenses, have an unrealistic and grandiose image of themselves. Step Four chops these grandiose aspects of our psyche down to size.

One of my big realizations and turning points in recovery was doing Step Four—and realizing what a complete self-centred jerk I had been, especially to those I cared for. I had a glamorized notion of my relationship with people while using—I thought they appreciated my chaos, as it made their dull lives exciting. Accidentally setting my girlfriend's arm on fire with gasoline, in an attempt to make some "artistic fire sculpture" after an all night cocaine binge, or asking her to shake my helmet every time I nodded off, due to a cocktail of heroin and barbiturates, while we are riding my motor bike, was not as much "fun" for her as I originally thought. Accessing my shadow in Step Four made me see that I was often a burden, a danger, and a massive annoyance to everyone I knew while I was in active addiction. This realization was a fatal blow to my misguided glamorous and grandiose rationalizations of my addiction.

Regardless of clean time, Step Four is a good spring cleaning of the psyche—especially the manner in which it deals with resentments. By looking at "our part" in resentments, we start owning our projections and may realize that the reason we resent the person, place, or event is that we have disowned the characteristic we resent in them in ourselves. It does not mean we endorse bad behavior; we merely realize that if we have an exaggerated emotional response to something, it strongly points to our shadow in action.

Step Ten, I believe, is a significantly underrated step. It is no secret that daily journaling can be a valuable process. Step Ten has often been referred to as a mini, daily Step Four: "We continued to take personal inventory and when we were wrong promptly admitted it."[100] Step Ten alerts us to aspects in our psyche before they become shadow. Let's say you had an argument with somebody—if you stay angry at them when you are going to bed, you go to bed with the idea that they are wrong. Tomorrow, or a couple of days later, you forget about it, and by then this low grade resentment goes and "lives" somewhere in your unconscious. As we know, to have resentments is actually denying something about ourselves. Unprocessed and unowned, these events add to our "shadow reservoir." By doing Step Ten at night, you process the incident, see if you played a part in it, or accept that they were wrong and that that is also okay. I think all compassion is based on the unspoken belief that we have that part in us towards which we are compassionate in others. We cannot have compassion towards something if we have completely disowned it in ourselves.

Step Ten is a daily exercise for our psychological health and helps us to prevent denial. Moreover, Step Ten provides daily insight into our perceptions and relationships with the world, ourselves, and others; in Step Ten, we explore whether or not our thinking is inaccurate. Some of us have life scripts that attract abusive people. Psychological health also means having the capacity to remove oneself from relationships with abusive people. This is where healthy boundaries come into play. Step Ten helps us to become more aware of the effect our daily environment has on our psychological health. Step Ten is also a good opportunity to list and observe what we have to be grateful for today. Step Ten has been an invaluable cornerstone in my recovery, and I still do it daily. The following two shadow/emotional practices can be incorporated into daily journaling.

The 3-2-1 Shadow Process

Ken Wilber's 3-2-1 Shadow Process is a simple yet powerful technique that you can incorporate into daily Step Ten journaling. This technique can also be applied in the here and now. This process is the distilled essence of shadow work that happens in many forms of psychotherapy. Seeing that resentments are the number one cause of relapse, this technique can prove invaluable—it is a powerful resentment buster. This practice is also useful when doing the resentment part of your Step Four. Apply this technique to each resentment.

The problem with resentments is that they take a huge amount of psychic energy and literally poison our body-mind. I often visualize resentment as a little man living in my psyche— the bigger the resentment the bigger his house. Some are so big, they even get married to other resentments and have children, and eventually they start planting crops and may even build a little village. Over time, your psyche may become densely occupied with theses villagers, harvesting the land of your psychic energy. After I completed the resentment part of my Step Four, it felt like my psyche was detoxed. I had all this new psychic land to inhabit with constructive and healthy populations. We cannot become psychologically well while hanging onto resentments; it cannot occur amongst villages of resentments. "Resentments are also underlined in the *Big Book* of Alcoholics Anonymous as the "number-one offender" that destroys more alcoholics than anything else. There resentment is seen as the major force behind recovering addicts' return to their addiction. From resentment stems all form of spiritual disease."[101]

There are two ways to recognize your shadow. First, it is that which "makes you negatively hypersensitive, easily triggered, reactive, irritated, angry, hurt, or upset. Or it may keep coming up as an emotional tone or mood that pervades your life."[102] Another way to describe it is that which "makes you positively hypersensitive, easily infatuated, possessive, obsessed, overly attracted, or perhaps it becomes an ongoing idealization that structures your motivation or mood."[103] It is important to know that our shadow not only contains repressed negativity, but also the positive aspects of ourselves that we do not acknowledge. Becoming aware of this "positive" shadow material is also very valuable.

The 3-2-1 Shadow process has three simple steps.[104] In the book *Integral Life Practice,* Ken Wilber et al. describe the 3-2-1

Shadow Process as follows:

3—Face it

The first step is to closely observe whatever is upsetting to you. Write it down factually using a 3rd person perspective.

2—Talk to it

The next step is to begin a dialogue with the disturbance. Ask questions and allow it to respond back to you. Write it down or vocalize it.

1—Be it

The final step is to speak or write as the actual disturbance using 1st person pronouns like "I", "me," or "mine." Then make the statement, "I am _____" or "_____ is me." "This, by nature, will almost always feel very discordant or "wrong." After all, it's exactly what your psyche has been very busy denying! But try it on for size, since it contains at least a kernel of truth. To complete the process, let the previously excluded reality register, not just abstractly but on multiple levels of your being. This engenders a shift in awareness, emotions, and subtle energy that frees up the energy and attention that was taken up by your denial."[105]

Mindfulness of Your Current Emotion

This technique originated from Dialectic Behavior Therapy (DBT). "DBT is a broad-based cognitive behavioral treatment developed specifically for Borderline Personality Disorder," but it is also used with many other populations like adolescents and addicts.[106] DBT uses psychosocial skills training in group and lecture settings and is clinically proven to be very effective. I have used it with great success in a clinical environment with addicts. One of the modules of DBT focuses on emotional regulations skills. The technique I will describe below is from that module.

According to DBT, painful emotions are part of the human condition. DBT assumes there are valid reasons for these painful emotions. It assumes further that we cannot get rid of them and therefore, the only real option is to find ways of relating to emotions so that they do not induce unnecessary suffering. It suggests that the way to do this is to accept them. This is in line with the principles of mindfulness, the core module in DBT. The psychosocial skill of "mindfulness of your current emotion" comprises four simple steps—simple, but powerful.

1. **Observe Your Emotion**

    Just note the presence of the emotion. Step back and recognize what is arising. It is also useful to name it. Say to yourself, I am experiencing _____ right now.

2. **Experience Your Emotion**

    Do not suppress or block the emotion. Rather experience it with all its accompanied bodily sensations. Feel its presence in various parts of your body. Just experience it fully. Give yourself permission to feel it, whatever it is.

3. **Remember: You are Not Your Emotion**

    Do not necessarily act on the emotion. Remind
    yourself that this too shall pass, that you are
    more than your feelings, and that this is merely
    something that is happening to you—it is not you.
    You can also remember times when you have felt
    differently to remind yourself that this current
    feeling will pass.

4. **Practice Loving Your Emotion**

    Don't judge your emotion—accept that this is what
    is happening now, and say to yourself, it is okay. Do
    not enter into self-talk about the appropriateness of
    the emotion. Practice loving your current emotion by
    accepting it.[107]

The purpose of this simple technique is not to avoid acting
responsibly relative to the emotion, but to give you greater clarity,
thereby allowing you to act in the best possible way. Much of our
suffering results from secondary emotions. These are emotions
resulting from our response to the emotions we experience, such
as feeling shame that we are angry, or angry that we are scared.
By totally accepting your emotion first, and experiencing it
without judgment, you can act responsibly. Addicts often have
labile emotions that are not necessarily connected to reality. More
often than not, the best thing to do is not to act but rather to ride
them out. Using the phrase "this too shall pass" is a powerful
mantra to repeat in emotionally distressing episodes. The more
we learn to sit with difficult feelings without acting destructively
or medicating them, the less power they hold over us in the future

and consequently, the less we suffer. This technique can also be applied when experiencing strong emotions while meditating.

Rational Emotive Behavior Therapy

Rational Emotive Behavior Therapy (REBT) is a therapy and self-help technique developed by Albert Ellis. It is based on the assumption that our feelings are caused by the way we think and interpret a situation. This is a very simple self-help technique when used properly. It increases emotional intelligence and decreases emotional vulnerability, creating greater self-efficacy. REBT is particularly useful for us addicts because, as a population, we often have distorted thinking. REBT gives us the opportunity to challenge our faulty thinking, which results in a more mature emotional life.

Have you ever done something in the heat of the moment that you regret? Of course! Now especially for those of us with addictions or emotional problems, situations like this may happen so often that our lives seem to be out of control. "Sometimes our upset feelings lead to self-defeating behavior, negative results, more upset feelings, more self-defeating behavior, and so on into a vicious cycle."[108]Addicts are profoundly emotionally illiterate, especially when it comes to accurately recognizing and naming negative feelings. Unpleasant feelings will normally fall into one of the four following categories: bad (ashamed, guilty); mad (annoyed, enraged, furious, hostile, irritated); sad (depressed, grief-stricken, hurt, lonely, miserable); and scared (afraid, anxious, frightened, nervous, panicky, terrified). Mostly, we believe that our feelings have external causes. The reality is that our feelings are caused more by our thoughts about events than by the events themselves. In the ABC process of REBT, your thoughts are the main factor causing and maintaining feelings. So it is what you think about an event, and not the event itself, that is mainly responsible for your happiness or unhappiness. To apply the ABC process, we describe the event (A); identify our upsetting thoughts (B); label our upset feelings (i.e., shame, anger, depression, anxiety), and then describe the actions we take because of them (C). Now we must dispute our thinking and replace inaccurate and negative thoughts with more realistic or positive thoughts (D). Finally, we set realistic reachable goals and take action (E). The REBT technique can be applied anytime and anywhere, but it is particularly useful when you are writing your daily diary. This provides you with an opportunity to rectify faulty thinking on a daily basis—or whenever necessary—before it becomes a resentment or a perpetual fear.

Therapy

It is common for recovering addicts to be in therapy at various stages of their recovery. I believe it is an essential aspect of a sustainable Integrated Recovery Lifestyle. The question is, which type of therapy is most appropriate for your current stage of recovery? The problem with therapy, in the context of recovery, is that certain types of therapy and/or therapists can become counterproductive to the recovery process. It is not unheard of that therapists who are unfamiliar with addiction have advised their clients that 1) controlled drinking or using is an option, 2) that they are not addicts in the first place, or 3) now that they have resolved the psychodynamic causes of their addiction, they are cured of it. These are extreme examples, but there are also less severe degrees of danger. For example, therapists working on trauma or family of origin issues too early in the recovery process may create such emotional turmoil that their client relapses.

Another danger that therapy presents for recovering addicts is that often individuals in recovery do so much therapy that they start equating therapy with recovery and, as we have seen, therapy is only one of many components. This attitude can create more self-obsession through constant morbid introspection. This is the "shadow side" of therapy. Another potential danger is that a considerable amount of therapists are unfamiliar with existing recovery theory and conditions like co-dependency and adult-child syndrome. My simple advice, to avoid the abovementioned dangers, is that you should only consult a therapist who is knowledgeable about addiction and up-to-date with contemporary recovery theory.

Recovering individuals require different therapies at different stages of recovery, because each stage presents its own set of unique challenges. Clearly, if you are ten years clean and married with kids, or if you are three months clean and fighting cravings, then the challenges that your life situation presents are different. Additionally, from a self-developmental perspective, as we progress to new and higher levels of personal development, new needs and potential pitfalls arise. Shadow work is required at each new stage. A question remains, what type of therapy is optimal at your current level of personal development? This is a complex issue and beyond the scope of this book. For those interested in exploring this issue further, I recommend Wilber's book *Integral Psychology* and Mark Forman's book, *A Guide to Integral Psychotherapy*.

In our previous discussion of stages of development, I pointed out that our different lines of development take place through a range of stages that can be classified in many ways. A simple stage model was presented comprising three stages: pre-personal, personal, and supra-personal, or egocentric, ethnocentric, and worldcentric. Each of these stages has its own range of potential pathologies. The beauty of using a developmental approach to therapy is that it provides the ability to choose a therapy that is most appropriate for the stage of development you are experiencing difficulties with. Different types of therapy are stronger at certain stages of development. For instance, existential therapy is more relevant for the pathologies in higher levels of development dealing with meaning of life issues than for pathologies in lower levels of development dealing with personality disorders.Using a developmental approach, we—or with our therapist—can decide on the type of therapy that will be most effective for our present issues. Wilber writes, "So it is not that a given therapy applies to one narrow wave of development, but that, in focusing on one or two waves, most forms of therapy increasingly lose their effectiveness when applied to more distant realms."[109]

Healthy Boundaries

An aspect of psychological health that is worth mentioning, and that provides a balance to our discussion so far, relates to boundaries. Psychological health does not only mean that our inner worlds are stable and healthy, but also that we relate to others and the world in healthy ways. For that, we need healthy boundaries. Most addicts have problems with their boundaries— either too rigid or too porous. Unhealthy boundaries can have either pathological masculine (too rigid) or pathological feminine (too porous) features. Depending on the nature of a relationship, we can switch from one to the other. Nowhere are pathological boundaries exemplified more poignantly than in the myth of Narcissus and Echo.

In the myth, Echo, the fairest of the wood nymphs, has been struck speechless by Hera, Zeus' jealous wife. From that point forward, Echo cannot speak other than to repeat what others say. Echo is therefore unable to declare her love for handsome Narcissus, and follows him about, hoping he will notice her. Finally, she finds him alone, calling out to his friends, "Is anyone there?" Thrilled, but too shy to meet him face-to-face, Echo instead remains hidden behind a tree and calls back, "Here . . . here!" Narcissus looks but sees no one. "Come," he shouts. This is what Echo has been waiting for, and stepping forward, she beckons to Narcissus and says sweetly, "Come." But Narcissus turns away in disgust from her outstretched arms, and says, "I will die before I give you power over me," to which Echo responds forlornly, "I give you power over me."

His rejection leaves her feeling ashamed. She cannot be comforted, yet she continues to love Narcissus. Nemesis, the goddess of righteous anger, enraged at the way Narcissus has treated Echo, arranges for him to lean over a pool one day and fall hopelessly in love with his own reflection. Thereafter, Narcissus slowly dies of a broken heart, unable to get any affectionate response from his own image. Upon his death, Echo slowly turns to stone—yet still we hear her voice in the canyons, forever repeating what other people say.[110]

In the myth, Narcissus represents the pathological masculine with over-rigid boundaries, and Echo represents the pathological feminine with weak or no boundaries; or, this can be understood as unhealthy/archaic narcissism and co-dependence.

This myth also points out how certain types are attracted to each other. When your friendships, work relationships, or romantic relationships are characterized by either one of these unhealthy extremes, you need to take note and get the appropriate help. Many addicts, once clean, tend to find themselves on the other side of the street and are now attracted to others with narcissistic conditions and/or addictions.

After extensive therapy, we often tend to look at our part in all situations and think we are capable of dealing with any situation or person if we remain psychologically healthy and keep our side of the street clean. And yes, this is true to a large extent, but when we find ourselves in relationships with really unhealthy people or institutions, no amount of individual therapy will necessarily resolve our difficulties. The reality is that there are certain situations, institutions, and people that, regardless of the psychological work we do, will always cause us great distress for whatever reasons. Sometimes the best form of "therapy" is simply to avoid or leave the person, situation, or institution.

Living in Consultation

Finally, I want to add what I believe to be the most important emotion regulation skill—living in consultation. When you are in profound crisis and the wheels really come off, many of the above emotion regulation skills don't work that well—you need the big guns. I have found that the most powerful crisis survival skill and emotion regulation skill is to spend time with people that care for me. By being around them, with their love, support, and advice, almost any painful situation is bearable. This is where 12-step fellowships have so much to offer. So if you find yourself in an emotional crisis in any stage of recovery, regardless of what practices you are pursuing, spending time with those that love and care for you is often essential to metabolize the experience.

Designing the Psychological Recovery Dimension of your IRP

An adequate level of health in your psychological recovery dimension is essential. Chronic unresolved and unattended emotional suffering will eventually lead to relapse, some destructive pathology, or another addiction. Remember, you will always have some shadow and neuroses—that is the human condition. Our aim is not to be completely free of it all, but to function with a certain degree of psychological health, so that we can live relatively productive and happy lives. The components of your psychological recovery dimension are:

- Step Ten—daily journal
- Individual therapy
- Group therapy
- Feelings work

The following suggestions and exercises will help you design and choose the appropriate practices, which will ensure that your psychological recovery dimension is functioning adequately.

1. Daily journal (Step Ten): Are you writing your daily journal? Are you incorporating techniques like the 3-2-1 Shadow Process or REBT in your daily diary? Are you exploring your day from a psychological point of view;

looking for possible resentments and faulty thinking that leads to certain dysfunctional and inaccurate emotional responses? Explore what aspects of your daily diary you can improve upon. Remember, the purpose is not to write a short story every night, because you will probably not be able to keep up this practice. Rather, it is to cultivate a short routine that incorporates a brief perspective of your inner world on a daily basis.

2. Therapy: Are you in therapy? Is your current therapeutic process working for you? Do you feel this is the type of therapy that you need right now? If not, or if you are not seeing a therapist, what do you think you need? Have you discussed your therapeutic process with your sponsor? Is your therapist knowledgeable about addiction and recovery? If you cannot afford therapy, can you make a plan to make the money? Is there a therapy group you can join? (We will discuss this issue in more depth within the social recovery dimension.)

3. How are you currently feeling regarding your emotional and psychological health? Do you feel you need to do more step work? If you are experiencing emotional problems, is it related to another aspect of your other recovery dimensions, such as not sleeping enough or not attending meetings? Remember, deficiencies in any other recovery dimension will first be felt in your psychological dimension. So, if this recovery dimension is experienced as turbulent, it may also be the influence of a deficiency in another dimension. The psychological recovery dimension can be seen as your recovery thermostat.

CHAPTER 6
THE EXISTENTIAL RECOVERY DIMENSION

*Addiction, whatever its form, has always been
a desperate search, on a false and hopeless
path, for the fulfillment of human freedom.*

~ Medard Boss

Addicts will often tell you that their initial attraction to drugs was directly related to the perceived meaningless of their lives, and how drugs and drug culture provided an "instant" sense of meaning. As Luigi Zoja says, "[o]ne often turns to drugs because of the insignificance, senselessness, and flatness of one's present life, a dead and senseless thing fuelled solely by reflex action."[111]

Many existentially oriented (the word existential refers to or relates to existence—especially human existence) philosophers and psychologists believe that the search for meaning is the primary need that humans have. Viktor Frankl, psychiatrist and founder of Logotherapy, says a human being's most basic motivation is to find meaning in life. Frankl asserts "A cause, a reason, 'a certain why,' an aim, an ideal, or a purpose in the sense of an orientation towards a goal for which one devotes one's energies and time."[112] He believes other motivations are secondary to this primary motivation, and lack of such purpose leads to a sense of frustration, emptiness, and, in some cases, addiction. This idea has been echoed by psychologists like Irvin Yalom: "The human being seems to require meaning. To live without meaning, goals, values, or ideals seems to provoke considerable distress;"[113] and proto-existential philosopher Friedrich Nietzsche: "He who has a why to live can bear with almost any how."[114]

In conjunction with the desire for meaning, Frankl highlights the responsibility of the individual to find meaning in life. The relationship between freedom and responsibility is discussed throughout existential literature. This emphasis on freedom and responsibility, two central concepts in understanding addiction, has consequently led many researchers and clinicians to explore addiction, as well as recovery, from an existential framework. Empirical studies support an association between lack of meaning in life and mental health problems[115] and highlight the relationship between poor purpose and meaning in life and heavy alcohol use.[116] Furthermore, reported levels of purpose in life increased after individuals received treatment for their substance abuse problems, and it was found that individuals who experienced an increase of life purpose were less likely to relapse.[117]

The existential recovery dimension of an Integrated Recovery Lifestyle, which addresses this need for meaning, is one of its most vital aspects, because we can exist on need and duty for only so long, but without meaning, we are doomed to a dreary existence. If our recovery does not provide adequate meaning, we often gravitate back to the meaning provided by drugs. A Integrated Recovery Lifestyle is ultimately about striving for a fulfilled and meaningful life. The aim is to become the person we truly want to be, within the boundaries of our unique limitations and potentials. Each of us has a unique meaning, and to be happy (according to the existentialists), we have a responsibility to find it and live it to the best of our ability. "You are also a uniquely constituted and very particular refraction of universal light," notes Ken Wilber, "a unique flavor of universal consciousness, a uniquely shaped embodiment of universal awareness and passionate life energy... The transpersonal manifests most fully through the personal. Thus, to awaken to the transcendental, we do not have to put ourselves through a process of erasing our uniqueness."[118]

From birth, society coerces us into certain generic roles and often forces us to sacrifice our uniqueness and individual talents. This may be a significant contributing factor to the development of addiction in some individuals. If you are an artist at heart and are forced to be an accountant, then you are likely to experience internal dissonance. This is also relevant for those who have been in recovery for many years and may even cause a relapse, because they try to squeeze themselves into a generic role that they do not fit but "think they should." Wilber illuminates this phenomenon, and says that "[t]here is a vitality, a life force, an energy, a quickening that is translated through you into action, and because there is only one of you in all time, this expression is unique. And if you block it, it will never exist through any other medium, and it will be lost. The world will not have it".[119]

As addicts, we are so used to mistrusting our impulses that we often lean toward the other extreme and live out of duty—not passion. For addicts who are passionate and sensitive people, this may prove fatal. Addicts tend to have a spirit that Nietzsche calls "dionysian;" it cannot be suppressed and needs to be channeled into healthy means of expression. As we saw in the discussion on positive psychology, a happy life is composed of a combination of a pleasurable, engaged, and meaningful life. When we apply our character strengths to serve something greater than ourselves, we are the happiest. I believe that just being a happy human being is a great service to the world. As the German writer and philosopher Johann Wolfgang Goethe beautifully states:

> When the sound and wholesome nature of man acts as an entirety, when he feels himself in the world as in a grand, beautiful, worthy and worthwhile whole, when this harmonious comfort affords him a pure, untrammelled delight: then the universe, if it could be conscious of itself, would shout for joy at having attained its goal and wonder at the pinnacle of its own essence and evolution. For what end is served by all the expenditures of suns and planets and moons, of stars and Milky Ways, of comets and nebula, for worlds evolving and passing away, if at last a happy man does not involuntarily rejoice in his existence.[120]

Frankl says there are three main routes or methods to finding meaning in our lives, regardless of environmental factors. He describes the first two by saying that "[m]en can give meaning to their lives by realizing what I call *creative values*, by achieving tasks. But they can also give meaning to their lives by realizing *experiential values*, by experiencing the Good, the True, and the Beautiful, or by knowing one single human being in all his uniqueness."[121] The third he describes as attitudinal values and states that "even a man who finds himself in the greatest distress, in which neither activity nor creativity can bring values to life, nor experience give meaning to it—even such a man can still give his life a meaning by the way he faces his fate, his distress. By taking his unavoidable suffering upon himself he may yet realize values."[122]

Creativity in Recovery

If you are in recovery and find that you do not have hobbies and meaningful activities, you need to work on this in the same earnest way that you work your steps. I often say to clients that learning how to play a musical instrument or pursue an artistic activity can have great significance for their recovery. Art has the alchemical gift of transmuting our base experiences into artistic gold. In early recovery, I played in a small band. Writing music and poetry gave my suffering meaning; it gave my pain a purpose, and that made it worthwhile. I still feel the same—if I cannot create, then I slowly wither. I have seen many recovering addicts slowly become more and more miserable from being super-responsible and neglecting to have fun or pursue their passions. This is a sad sight, and they often end up using because it feels better to be high and miserable than be straight and miserable.

From a Jungian perspective, there are many archetypes that make up our personality. One of these archetypes is the Lover—this is the part of our psyche that thrives on chaos and rapture. For addicts, this is often the part of our psyche that became pathological. Jungian analyst Linda Leonard, in her book *Witness to the Fire: Creativity and Addiction*, refers to the Lover as the Romantic and says the following:

> The Romantic is the most entrancing, yet dangerous figure in the psyche of the addict. If untransformed, the Romantic can draw us into death. Yet the Romantic can draw us also into creativity and towards spiritual transformation, for its energy takes us from the grip of the practical world into the "forbidden" unknown realms. The Romantic is the archetypal figure who wants absolute merger with the loved one, who longs to be "somewhere, over the rainbow" or to dissolve into the night sea to experience union with the infinite. When this desire to merge with the infinite possesses one's life and reduces it to the futility of insatiable longing alone, then romanticism has become an addiction. Bound by the longing that is insatiable and ultimately does not satisfy, the Romantic is behind all addiction. But behind the restless longing of the Romantic is the soul's thirst for the divine fire of creativity. Therein lies the possibility for transformation.[123]

When addiction is viewed from this perspective, we can see the significance an existential orientation has for recovery.

Addiction and the creative pursuit for union with the Absolute are two sides of the same coin. When addicts enter recovery, they have to control the "Lover," or the "Romantic," part of their psyche as it is very much out of control. Eventually we must find balance, because repressing any part of our psyche leads to trouble; the repressed aspect will always find pathological ways to express itself. I think the repressed "Lover" archetype often manifests itself in a recovering addict's relationships, when they do not find an existential or creative outlet for their chaos.

All creativity and transformation is born out of chaos. Without chaos there is no evolution or life. Most spiritual awakenings need a "chaotic" prelude. As early twentieth century American philosopher William James wrote, "all transforming spiritual experiences are nearly always founded on calamity and collapse."[124] The chaos and despair that addiction creates is fertile soil for authentic spiritual-existential transformation and awakening. Chaos is pregnant with unlimited potential. Of course, as addicts, we know what happens when chaos goes too far. We need some healthy chaos in recovery, where we can be spontaneous, childlike, creative, and let our hair down. Healthy ways to do this are finding transcendence through sports, dancing, rock concerts, creating and playing music, and other creative pursuits that allow spontaneity and transcendence of our normal states.

Spirituality

In a letter replying to Bill W.,[125] Carl Jung stated, "You see alcohol in Latin is "spiritus" and you use the same word for the highest religious experience as well as for the most depraving poison. The helpful formula therefore is: *spiritus contra spiritum*." What Jung suggested when he used the phrase "Spiritus contra Spiritum" is that at the heart of an effective "treatment" for alcoholism, there has to be a profound spiritual or existential transformation. This is the same message that Jung related much earlier to Edwin Throckmorton Thacher (Ebby T). This interpretation of Jung's message to Ebby T., together with the influence of the work of William James, as well as Bill Wilson's own spiritual or mystical experience, saw that the Twelve Steps developed at its core a spiritual way of life and practice.

In 12-step culture, spirituality is seen as an essential component. I do not want to underplay the usefulness or even necessity of spirituality in many people's lives, but I do not believe that spirituality is an essential need, but rather underlying it is an essential need—the need for meaning. The origin of the word enthusiasm gives us a glimpse into the existential relationship between meaning and spirituality. Spiritual teacher and author Eckhart Tolle writes, "The word *enthusiasm* comes from the ancient Greek—*en* and *theos,* meaning God. And the related word *enthousiazein* means 'to be possessed by a god.'"[126] Therefore, another way to frame the value and emphasis that the Twelve Steps place on spirituality is to see it as a path to meaning. As mentioned earlier in the book, what is curative about most spiritual practices is that they provide a sense of meaning to people's lives. In short, spiritual practices are an adjunct to our innate need for meaning.

I place a significant emphasis on spirituality and spiritual practice in this chapter, as this is the predominant "existential method" in 12-step culture. One way to frame it is that 12-step philosophy is spiritually pluralistic, which means that it allows its members to find meaning in any form of spirituality. On the other hand, I would call the Integrated Recovery approach "existentially pluralistic," which means that individuals are allowed to find meaning in any pursuit, including spirituality. The description and practices of spirituality described here are very useful for those on a more traditional spiritual path, but I do not think they are essential for recovery or for living a happy and authentic life. For those with an atheistic worldview, or for those not inclined toward traditional spiritual practice, any pursuit(s) that provides them with adequate meaning can be enough to satisfy their spiritual-existential needs. Yet many aspects of spiritual practice described here are useful, even for those with no spiritual inclination.

No aspect of 12-step philosophy is as misunderstood and misrepresented as its spiritual component. Before we can go on to have a meaningful discussion about spirituality, we first need to define it. This is necessary because chances are that your and my ideas about spirituality are different from everyone else's. In his book *Integral Spirituality*, Wilber states that there are four common meanings or definitions given to the word spiritual:

1) the highest levels in any of the lines;

2) a separate line itself;

3) an extraordinary peak experience or state;

4) a particular attitude.[127]

Another common use is for it to represent a belief in God or a guiding force or energy in the Cosmos. The definition of the word spiritual used in this book is a combination of some of the above-mentioned ones that fit in with an Integral view of the Twelve Steps. I define spirituality as "the quality of our relationships towards ourselves, others, and our being-in-the-world." This broad definition is in keeping with AA's pluralistic attitude and integral stance expressed in a "Higher Power of your understanding," as well as its humanistic view of spirituality as the application of "spiritual principles in our daily affairs." According to this definition, spirituality is always accessible in the here and now. According to our approach, addiction is viewed as a progressive process of isolation and fragmentation, whereas recovery is understood as a process of connection and wholeness. What always underlies any authentic spiritual or mystical experience is an increased sense of connection or union with Reality. The recovery process is thus seen as a set of methods to increase our connection with Reality or the Transcendent, or whatever we find meaningful-in-the-world.

Altered States

As we saw previously in our discussion about states, the recovery process needs to make room for the alteration of consciousness. As many scholars have pointed out, humans have an innate need to alter consciousness, and when a society does not provide healthy means of achieving altered states of consciousness (ASC), we will find unhealthy ways. Many scholars believe that one of the reasons there is such an increase in drug addiction in contemporary culture is the lack of healthy and culturally acceptable modes of ASC.[128] "The act of turning to drugs follows upon the need to transcend one's habitual state, and this unconsciously connects and unites the act with the religious urge or, to be more precise, with the aspirations of the mystic and his search for ecstasy."[129] Hence Jung's statement that alcoholics are misguided mystics. In this light, addiction is understood as a misguided attempt at mystical union. Addiction is therefore: "A mysticism in the absence of God, a mystical transport going nowhere... that is, a mysticism without mysticism or experience without truth."[130]

Michael Winkelman, an expert on the topic of substance abuse and ASC, believes that addicts often engage in the pursuit of ASC's, which is to be understood as a normal human motive, but they do this in self-destructive ways. He states that, "[t]he importance of an alteration of consciousness in substance abuse recovery is emphasized in the AA recovery process, which calls for "a new state of consciousness and being" designed to replace the self-destructive pursuit of alcohol-induced altered states with a positive life-enhancing approach. Standard approaches to addressing substance dependence have failed to consider the role of ASC in human nature or drug dependence."[131] There are many others who echo Winkelman's opinion that one of the main reasons why AA and other 12-step programs are so successful is that they acknowledge the need for a spiritual way of life and the need for sudden or gradual alteration of consciousness through activities like meditation, working the steps, and contemplation.[132] "The authentic search and re-union with our inner home is a genuine spiritual path. The false search is called addiction. Addiction is a mistaken path to the genuine impulse for a spiritual reawakening."[133]

It will be of great benefit to us to use an Integral framework to expand and inform our understanding of altered states as well as the spiritual experiences we encounter as a result of working an Integrated Recovery Program. Wilber uses a matrix called the "Wilber-Combs Lattice" to describe the range of possible spiritual or mystical experiences available to us. He states that we can have four types of spiritual or mystical experiences at any stage of development. Furthermore, we interpret our spiritual experiences in the context of our stage of development.

In the same way, depending on our stage of development, we will perceive and understand our Higher Power within our developmental context. This is a necessary insight for tolerance of others' beliefs. When having a deity mystical experience, a Hindu and a Christian will interpret it within their respective religious contexts. One might see a person on a cross, and the other a blue figure with an elephant head. If both are unaware of the socio-historical influence affecting their experience, they will argue that their experience is the only valid one. The informed person will know that neither view is right or wrong, but merely an interpretation of the experience in the context of one's level of development.

We are all aware of the problems religious people have caused throughout history: when interpreting their religious impulses at a mythic level, and mistakenly taking myth for fact, they then tried to impose these "facts" on others. This is why modernity attempted to reject mythic religions, French Enlightenment writer and philosopher Voltaire's battle cry was "Remember the cruelties!" and why Nietzsche said "God is dead." Nietzsche was saying that the mythic God was dead in the modern era—and rightly so.

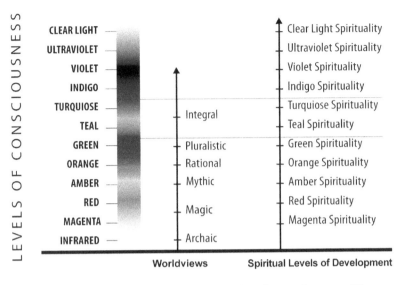

Figure 7: Spiritual Levels of Development[134]

As Wilber says, a mythic understanding of the Transcendent is appropriate up to the age of ten or so, but becomes really problematic when a thirty-year-old "adult" still believes the earth was created in six days and so forth. It is fine if a small portion of the population is operating from a mythic level, but it becomes really problematic when this is the dominant cultural mode—hence the unspeakable horrors of the Spanish Inquisition led by the Catholic Church in the name of a "loving" God. In this context, we see why it is of pragmatic value that the Twelve Steps are pluralistic in their stance regarding specific spiritual beliefs—hence the suggestion to choose a "God of your understanding." This is saying that whatever stage of development you are in, it is fine, as long as you work on your own spiritual development. If the Twelve Steps had specific spiritual beliefs, then by default it would become exclusive. Although 12-step programs remain "spiritually" neutral, they are often labeled as mythic organizations. This is an unfortunate misunderstanding; 12-step fellowships do have strong mythic elements, which I believe are necessary, but the principles and traditions of 12-step fellowships like NA and AA are certainly not mythic. Addicts in early recovery, who are often moving out of egocentric levels up the developmental ladder, need the healthy elements of conformity and rigidity of the mythic-conformist level. Twelve-step programs are accessible for all individuals regardless of their stage of development or belief system.[135]

Due to the destructive effect many of the world's mythic religions have had, and are still having, on the world, many individuals entering NA or AA are against any form of spiritual beliefs. Who can blame them? The problem is that they often throw the baby out with the bath water. A more technical term for this phenomenon is what Wilber calls a level/line fallacy. Because we mistake the erroneous beliefs of one level or stage with that of a whole line of development, we incorrectly assume the whole line is erroneous. For example, you grow up in a fundamentalist religious family and decide that they have it all wrong; then every time someone mentions God, or anything spiritual, you think they are as mistaken as the fundamentalist community you came from. And when you encounter a nondual Zen monk, and he talks about spirituality, you erroneously place what he says in the same class as a fundamentalist philosophy. The mythic is only one level of spirituality, which manifests all the way up the spectrum of development. Even though the great Taoist sage Lao Tzu and a Spanish Inquisitor burning somebody at the stake for growing parsley both have a conception of the Transcendent, it is obvious that one is much more developed than the other.[136]

There are four types of spiritual or mystical experiences that we can access at any given moment. Wilber explains: "To experience a oneness with all phenomenon in the gross-waking state is typical nature mysticism. To experience a oneness with all phenomenon in the subtle-dream state is typical deity mysticism. To experience a oneness with all phenomenon (or lack thereof) in the causal-unmanifested state is typical formless mysticism. To experience a oneness with all phenomenon arising in gross, subtle, and causal states is a typical nondual mysticism."[137]

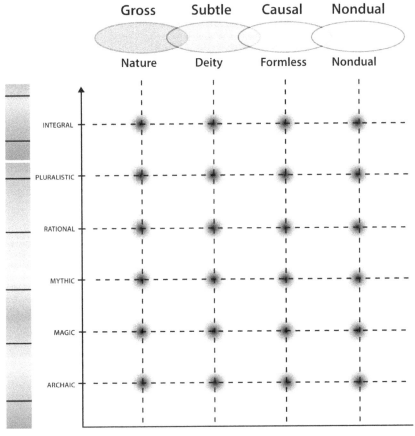

Figure 8: Wilber-Combs Lattice[138]

This may sound irrelevant for you in recovery, but it can prove to be very useful. Seeing that the basic text of AA states that instant spiritual or mystical experiences are frequent events, and that the ultimate aim of working a recovery program is to promote spiritual or existential awakening, it is clear that a deeper understanding of the nature of these peak or spiritual experiences can be very useful. Wilber states that when we have a peak experience, but do not have either the context or language to make sense of it, its effect is only temporary. But when we can somehow make sense of it, and place the experience within a cognitive framework, the effect is lasting.

A good example is the peak or mystical experience that Bill Wilson had while in hospital, which played such a pivotal role in the development of the Twelve Steps. Initially, after Wilson's mystical insight, he thought he had gone mad, but his doctor assured him that this was not the case and referred Wilson to the work of William James. When reading James' *Varieties of the Religious Experience,* which Ebby T. brought to Wilson in the hospital, he was able to place his own mystical experience within a context and make sense of it, thereby integrating the experience into a new view of Reality. How different matters might have been had Dr. Silkworth been of narrow insight and made light of Wilson's mystical insight or agreed with him that he had indeed gone mad! The Twelve Steps has its origin in a mystical experience and consequently promotes this type of experience. Joni Mountain, author of *The Joy Beyond Craving: A Buddhist Perspective on Addiction and Recovery*, states that "when the distinction between Higher Consciousness and ourselves disappears, it does so not because we absorb that Consciousness into ourselves, but because we put aside our illusory idea of "self" and become absorbed in the Divine Emptiness completely. This is the spiritual Awakening of which both Bill W. and the Buddha spoke."[139]

Three Perspectives of Spiritual Practice

Wilber and his colleagues at the Integral Institute believe that Spirit, the Transcendent, Universal Consciousness, God—call it what you like—manifests and is accessible in the three different perspectives that are available to us at any given instant: the 1st-, 2nd-, and 3rd-person perspectives. Historically, most spiritual and religious traditions have favored one or two perspectives, but seldom three. Wilber et al. believe that considering less than all three perspectives often leads to a fragmented and partial understanding. In our Integrated Recovery Program, we can choose to practice spirituality from all three perspectives. Incidentally, the Twelve Steps promotes all three as well. In the following section, I will investigate various spiritually oriented ways in which we can practice the existential recovery dimension. For those of you who choose not to have a spiritual practice or path, each of these 1st-, 2nd-, and 3rd-person practices can also be framed within a secular existential perspective. I will provide a description of a more secular approach at the end of each section.

Meditation (1st Person)

Step Eleven of AA states: "Through prayer and meditation we…" As we can see, the Twelve Steps is no stranger to meditation. Step Eleven is probably the most underutilized of the Twelve Steps, because the word meditation is open to interpretation and, unfortunately, often uninformed interpretation. If you truly want to work Step Eleven, it is suggested you meditate. Moreover, the basic text of AA states, "It is easy to let up on the spiritual program of action and rest on our laurels… What we really have is a daily reprieve contingent on the maintenance of our spiritual condition."[140] You might have noticed the phrases "spiritual program of action" and "maintenance." If you ask people in recovery what their daily spiritual practice is, you will probably find very little evidence of actual practice, although the basic text of AA explicitly states "maintenance" of a daily spiritual practice. All authentic spiritual paths promote some form of meditation, not just in the East but also commonly in Western contemplative traditions. Simply put, if you want an authentic spiritual life, then it is strongly suggested that you meditate or participate in a contemplative spiritual practice. In our discussion on mindfulness, I expounded many of the virtues of meditation, in particular mindfulness meditation, so I will not do so again but will briefly expand on the mechanism of meditation and why it is of particular benefit to us in recovery.

Addiction is characterized by egocentricity, a constricted awareness, and self-centered denial. At the core of the recovery process, however, is a gradual expansion of awareness that progressively includes the perspectives of others as well as greater insight into our lives and behavior. According to Wilber, meditation can increase vertical stage development by two stages in only four years. There is no single practice or therapy that can claim this. Wilber explains why meditation has the capacity to promote tremendous vertical growth. "When you meditate, you are in effect witnessing the mind, thus turning subject into object—which is exactly the core mechanism of development (the subject of one stage becomes the object of the next)."[141] When meditating, we observe our thoughts, perceptions, and emotions without getting overly attached to them; we merely witness—and therefore they become the objects of our awareness. Over time, therefore, what was once the subject of our awareness becomes the object of our awareness and, as Wilber explains, this is the mechanism by which we grow developmentally. By observing our thoughts and feelings mindfully, we may start to realize their fleeting nature, and we may start taking them less seriously. Consequently, they lose some of their power over us, giving us the freedom to choose how we respond to our thoughts. This property of meditation is particularly useful for addicted populations, as a fundamental feature of addiction is the presence of erroneous and self-destructive thoughts and self-talk.

Another feature of meditation that is really beneficial for recovering addicts is that "meditation increases ego strength."[142] Ego strength in the psychiatric sense means the "capacity for disinterested witnessing."[143] Addiction is often characterized by weak ego strength—a feature of borderline and narcissistic disorders. In the addict, "the self is not differentiated from the world, there is no strong ego, and thus the world is treated as an extension of the self, 'egocentrically'... only with the emergence of a mature ego does egocentrism die down!"[144] That is why they say in AA that at the core of alcoholism is self-centeredness. Consequently, recovery is about becoming less self-centered, which requires a strong and mature ego. Meditation is therefore especially useful in recovery, because "meditation is one of the single strongest antidotes to egocentrism and narcissism."[145] It is inaccurate to see meditation as moving beyond the ego or aiming at becoming egoless. This would cause developmental regression and bolster egocentricity. Meditation aims at transcendence while including a strong ego. In "New Age" circles, the word ego is often associated with all that is bad and selfish in the human condition. But it is not the ego that is bad and causes selfishness—rather a lack of a strong differentiated ego.

There are many meditation practices. One of the simplest and most frequently used practices in mindfulness circles is the basic breath meditation. In the book *Integral Life Practice,* the authors describe, "breath meditation is one of the most elegant combinations of the two meditative capacities simultaneously: mental focus and open awareness. Concentration trains mental focus and stability, while open awareness relaxes, expands, and releases this mental focus into a free encounter with every present moment. Breath meditation thus stands at the border between formless and form-based types of meditation."[146]

Meditation is only truly effective when done regularly, but it can be really difficult to keep up the practice. It is useful to set yourself a realistic practice goal. Start with ten minutes a day and build up to twenty or thirty minutes a day, or twice a day. Even better, join a meditation group or spiritual community that holds regular meditation practice sessions and meditation retreats. I strongly suggest going on an eight-week Mindfulness-Based Stress Reduction course and reading Jon Kabat-Zinn's books. Mindfulness is also about being compassionate with yourself, so if you skip a day, week, or month, then be kind to yourself and begin again "just for today."

Another way you can speed things up and make meditation practice easier is by using brainwave entrainment technology (BWE), like the downloadable or CD tracks created by iAwake Technologies.[147] Some CDs are merely designed for their immediate effect to create altered states, whereas others, like the Profound Meditation Program or Holosync®, focus on long-term effects on brain metabolism, structure, and functioning. Brainwave entrainment uses binaural beats, which entrain your brain from normal waking states down to deep, meditative states, which correspond to slower brainwave frequencies. The latter are normally only accessed through very advanced levels of meditation. Our normal waking consciousness is the beta brainwave state, and BWE guides the brain from beta to either alpha, theta, or delta states.[148] Using BWE CDs that use isochronic beats has the further benefit of not requiring earphones and can be played on a hi-fi. This technology can therefore easily be used with a group of people.

I used isochronic beats every morning in a treatment center with my clients and was always amazed that they could sit for twenty minutes with no problem due to the BWE. I strongly recommend using BWE CDs when you start a meditative practice. Apart from the fact that listening to these CDs helps one to meditate, they also have a large number of other physiological and psychological benefits that will enhance every aspect of your Integrated Recovery Lifestyle. John Dupuy says that "binaural meditation can be combined with traditional meditative practices, such as following the breath or self inquiry, in order to create a more synergistic effect. In the case of the recovering addict, this is extremely important, as they do not have the luxury of waiting two to five years to start seeing results.[149]

A Secular Understanding of 1st-Person Spiritual/Existential Practice

The mindfulness-based stress reduction program developed by Jon Kabat-Zinn is a secular approach to mindfulness meditation and therefore useful for those looking for a secularly oriented form of meditation practice. I strongly recommend a formal and consistent meditation practice, whether your recovery program is spiritually or secularly oriented, as either way, meditation is a very useful practice.

Communion (2nd Person)

A 2nd-person perspective of spirituality can be understood as the relationship you have with your Higher Power. "It is a profound and paradoxical matter to turn and face the Unfathomable Mystery of Existence. How is it possible? How can you face the Ultimate, Unlimited, Almighty, and Omnipresent?"[150] When Step Eleven speaks about "conscious contact with God," it is referring to this direct, relational aspect of spiritual practice—also referred to as communion. Wilber often points out that without 2nd-person communion, 1st-person spiritual practice may actually reinforce self-centeredness. In other words, 1st-person practice not tempered by 2nd-person practice reinforces narcissism—and 2nd-person practice prevents this.

Second-person spirituality is about humility and realizing our ultimate existential condition—that we are not God. This "waters down" our 1st-person realization that we are inseparable from the Ultimate. In the West, due to our many bad experiences with fundamental religions that overemphasize 2nd-person practice, we consider all forms of 2nd-person practice to be superficial. This is once again a level/line fallacy. Without existential humility, we exaggerate our self-importance, and this arrogance is what addiction thrives on. It takes great spiritual insight and maturity to live with the paradox of our existence: that from an ultimate perspective we are "divine," but from a relative perspective we are virtually insignificant. Spiritual immaturity causes us to see everything in black and white and consequently, we choose only one perspective.

How do we practice 2nd-person spirituality? The most common form is prayer. Your spiritual beliefs and conception of a Higher Power will define your conception and method of prayer. The Twelve Steps has an interesting slant on prayer, it states "… praying only for knowledge of His will for us and the power to carry that out." This is a truly Zen perspective. What Step Eleven is insinuating is that we accept Reality as it happens to us, and our "prayer" is that we will be happy regardless of the outcome. We stop controlling, start living in the moment, and accept life's outcomes. If we think about it pragmatically, life happens regardless of our intentions and desires. The only truly sane way to live is to stop clinging to our unrealistic desires and to make friends with whatever happens in the here and now. This is the essence of Step Eleven.

I have always thought petitioning prayer for an object or desired result is incredibly egocentric, for this assumes that the whole Universe will adjust itself to one's wishes. This is like a five-year-old expecting Santa Claus to fly all the way from the North Pole to personally deliver his presents. As Ralph Waldo Emerson, American essayist and poet, put it, "But prayer as a means to effect a private end is meanness and theft. It supports dualism and not a unity in nature and consciousness."[151] Step Eleven warns against such foolishness. In the *It Works: How and Why* of NA it states, "Though the temptation to pray for a particular result may be great, we must resist the urge to do so if we want to experience the rewards of the Eleventh Step. Praying for specific solutions to specific problems is not the answer."[152]

An interesting and creative way to view prayer is that it involves communion through presence with the Ultimate. Father Thomas Keating uses an analogy for this type of prayer; it is like an elderly married couple, sitting on a porch, not talking, but merely being in each other's presence. They are communicating, but without words. From this perspective, prayer is openness to the Ultimate, and as we start realizing our inseparableness and interrelationship with All That Is, our communion with Reality strengthens. Praying for knowledge of our Higher Power's will for us is asking for a *kensho* or *satori* or an authentic awakening, not for some personal divine plan and cosmic intervention, but for us to awaken to the true nature of immediate reality.

A Secular Understanding of 2nd-Person Practice:

A simple way to understand 2nd-person practice from a secular-existential point of view is to describe it as the way we relate to the world, or more particularly with the person/object we find meaningful. For example, if playing the guitar or a special person in your life provides you with meaning, there is a subject-object relationship between you and playing the guitar or between you and the person. A 2nd-person practice can be understood simply as the quality and experience of this relationship.

To further understand 2nd-person practice from a secular or existential perspective, it is useful to turn to existential philosopher Martin Heidegger's notion of "being-in-the-world." "Being-in-the-world" is Heidegger's substitute for terms such as subject, object, consciousness, and world. Heidegger believed that splitting things into subjects or objects, like we find in Western tradition and language, must be overcome, because all consciousness is consciousness of something—there is no consciousness separate from an object, and there is always a "mood" present in these relationships. A "mood" originates neither from the subject or the object but arises from being-in-the-world. It is only with a "mood" that are we allowed to encounter things in the world. Second-person practice is then understood as the "quality" of this mood (similar to the earlier definition of spirituality). Therefore 2nd-person practices seek for an "authentic mood," presence, or "attitude" toward what we find meaningful-in-the-world. Simply put, by having the right or authentic attitude toward what we find meaningful, we can encounter the person/object with greater and more fulfilled meaning.

From the 12-step perspective, this "mood" or "existential attitude" is described in its notion of spiritual principles. A pivotal aspect of 12-step philosophy is applying spiritual principles in our daily lives. I believe this element of the Twelve Steps is one of its most powerful and transformative practices—focusing on the quality of our attitude towards ourselves, others, and our being-in-the-world. When one's "mood' or "existential attitude" is guided by spiritual principles or attitudes, it leads to more authentic experience and meaning-in-the-world. As discussed earlier, positive psychology, with its 6 virtues and 24 character assets, further deepens our understanding of these spiritual principles. An applied spiritual principle often becomes part of our character, and our characters are therefore transformed by the application of spiritual principles.

Contemplation (3rd Person)

In 3rd-person spiritual practice, also referred to as contemplation, we engage with the Ultimate objectively—we contemplate the Ground of All Being. By studying, discussing, and contemplating philosophical, recovery, and spiritual texts, we strengthen our 3rd-person, or contemplative, spiritual practice. Doing written step work and reading about the steps deepens our spiritual insight. Going to workshops or joining a spiritual, recovery, or philosophical group discussion all contribute to our contemplative spiritual practice.

I strongly recommend the further study of Integral Theory, because it is a psychoactive map, in the sense that it augments your body-mind to become aware of a more nuanced and comprehensive view of reality. Integral Theory also provides incredible insight into spiritual issues, as spiritual philosophy is currently a minefield of contradictory information and "New Age" nonsense. A less obvious but equally powerful way to practice spiritual contemplation is expression through art, as discussed earlier in this chapter. Many spiritual traditions have a strong artistic component. For instance, Zen and its artistic expression are nearly inseparable.

A Secular Understanding of 3rd-Person Practice

The study, contemplation, and discussion of meaning and what you find meaningful are a powerful practice. From this perspective, studying any topic that you find meaningful is considered 3rd-person practice. Those with an atheistic or secular worldview may find studying existential philosophy and psychology literature useful, as it provides many different ways of understanding the world and our place in it.

Sangha

Joining a spiritual community or *sangha* is, in many cases, of great benefit to your spiritual life. Like with any practice and path, receiving guidance from those familiar with the path and practice is very helpful and accelerates your progress. Being part of a community can help you find a spiritual teacher who can further assist you in your spiritual pursuits. It is advisable to find a teacher familiar with addiction and recovery. Some teachers may disagree with an abstinence-based lifestyle, and because a spiritual teacher can be very influential, this may be dangerous to your recovery. Ken Wilber says "[a] truly awakened teacher can be an immense source of guidance, wisdom, and spiritual transmission.[153] The same advice goes for those who have a secular understanding of recovery. Joining a philosophy group or becoming part of the Integral community provides a sense of connection with like-minded individuals and necessary information and support to guide your particular journey. Even joining a band or sports team can have all the benefits of a spiritual sangha.

Designing the Existential Recovery Dimension of Your IRP

I will now provide some exercises that will help you design the existential dimension of your Integrated Recovery Program. The suggested components for your existential recovery dimension are:

- 1st-person spiritual/existential practice—meditation
- 2nd-person spiritual/existential practice—communion
- 3rd-person spiritual/existential practice—contemplation and study

The following suggestions and exercises will help you design and choose the appropriate practices to ensure that your existential recovery dimension is functioning adequately.

1. 1st-Person Meditation: Do you have a meditation practice? If so, when and for how long do you meditate? What type of meditation are you practicing? Are your meditation goals realistic? Do you feel the need to join a formal meditation group, and what groups are available in your area? Do you have enough information on meditation practice? If not, list some books or workshops you can read or join that will give you the information you need.

2. 2nd-Person Communion: Do you have a prayer life? If not, how can you improve on it? If you do not pray in the conventional sense of the word, then how do you strengthen your relationship with your Higher Power? Remember, there are many creative ways to "pray." If you are having trouble with this concept, speak to your sponsor or spiritual teacher about it. What is the "mood" or quality of your relationship with what you find meaningful-in-the–world? Are you putting your existential/spiritual life into practice? Are you practicing your spiritual principles in all your affairs? Make two lists, one in which you list the spiritual principles that you practice regularly, and the other in which you list all the spiritual principles you struggle with. Are you listing in your daily diary the spiritual principles you do and do not practice?

3. 3rd-Person Contemplation: How are you increasing your cognitive understanding of your personal spiritual or existential beliefs and practices? What books are

you reading? Are you part of a discussion group? Are there workshops or lectures you can attend to increase your insight?

4. Existential: Is your life currently meaningful; is this the life you want? If not, what can you do about it? List everything that you find meaningful in your life. What are the activities you love and find meaningful but that you are not practicing? If you are having trouble in this area, speak to your sponsor, therapist, and/or spiritual teacher about it. Remember the words of Goethe: "Whatever you can do or dream you can do, you must begin it. Boldness has genius, power, and magic in it."

5. Do you have any reservations about the existential component of your IRP? If so, have you discussed them with your sponsor, therapist, or spiritual teacher? What aspects of your spiritual/existential practice are under-evolved? What can you do about it?

6. Do you feel the need to join a spiritual or philosophical community? If so, is there a spiritual/philosophical community or meditation center near you? Remember, you can also communicate via the internet. If and when you take your spiritual practice more seriously, I strongly advise that you find a spiritual teacher. If you feel the need for a spiritual teacher, is there anybody you have in mind? If you are already working with a spiritual teacher, then is it working well for you? If not, is there somebody else you can draw on? If you are

not part of a spiritual or philosophical community, are there other groups you can join that share an interest in your passions?

CHAPTER 7
THE SOCIAL RECOVERY DIMENSION

Drug addiction is not, as generally believed, an escape from society, but a desperate attempt to occupy a place in it. Insofar as the addict perceives that his family is revolving hypnotically around him and that society is judging his behavior as an attack on civic unity, he will always remain homo oeconomicus while playing out his societal role as the negative hero. It is almost impossible for many young people to feel in any way useful in today's society. Why should we be so amazed that so many take drugs, and why should we interpret addiction as a regressive renunciation of the ego when the person making this choice is actually seeking a few moments of heroic identity? The archaic necessity of identifying both heroes and enemies becomes concentrated in the addict's creeping sensation of living a kind of civil war between a minority faction, made up of angels of death, and a stronger majority of law-abiding citizens. The latter, however, seem to lack any identity of their own.[154]

~ Luigi Zoja

It is crucial to understand drug use within a broader sociocultural context, as indicated in the above quote from Jungian analyst Luigi Zoja in his book, *Drugs, Addiction and Initiation: The Modern Search for Ritual.* Drug use and addiction is not merely about the psychoactive chemical properties and effects of the drug, but is interlinked with and inseparable from a much wider and complex cultural phenomenon. The self-medication hypothesis, which states that individuals use drugs to relieve inner pain, has great merit, but it is only part of the picture. William White, in his book *Pathways: From the Culture of Addiction to the Culture of Recovery,* writes that "[t]he culture of addiction is a way of life, a means of organizing one's daily existence, and a way of viewing people and events in the outside world. It is a way of talking, walking, dressing, gesturing, believing, mating, working, playing, thinking, and seeing that separates people who are "in the life" from those who are not. The culture of addiction encompasses values, artefacts, places, rituals, relationships, symbols, music, and art, all of which reinforce one's involvement in excessive drug consumption.[155]

Very few non-addicts can comprehend the brotherhood, sense of belonging, and purpose that certain addiction cultures provide. Speaking from my own experience, the camaraderie I felt with many of my fellow heroin addicts, the debauched sense of our uniqueness and freedom, gave me a great feeling of pride in being part of a group of "anti-heroes." On the measure of pleasure, normal life simply cannot compete with drug highs. When framing the drug high within a culture that condones, glorifies, and provides meaning for this behavior, the drug experience is further amplified by an existential and near religious component. Addiction is not just about being miserable, alone in a dark room using, because you are in pain, as junkies are often portrayed. It is also about freedom, pushing the boundaries to the limit, meaning, beauty, love, and brotherhood, and many other healthy values and needs—but framed in a destructive cultural expression. Unfortunately for the addict, while the drug culture provides all these benefits in the short term, it is not sustainable and nearly always comes at a great cost in the long run.

Often the brotherhood among addicts is the same as the camaraderie that soldiers feel alongside of each other in battle and war. In both of these contexts, the level of intimacy far exceeds normal boundaries, and in both worlds we walk with our friend's blood on our hands. Danger and fear create very strong bonds. The deeper one is drawn into the drug culture, the more distant and strange the "straight world" appears. What many addicts entering recovery—like soldiers coming back from a war—find the most difficult is the cultural transition. As with soldiers with Post Traumatic Stress Disorder (PTSD), who, on an emotional level, feel they are still fighting a war, addicts suffer similar PTSD symptoms and may feel like they are still in the trenches of addiction. It is through this framework that they interpret all reality. It took me years to see a spoon as a utensil to eat soup with, as opposed to a tool to cook heroin with. For the junkie, every experience of reality is affected and colored by the traumatic battle of addiction.

Drug use and addiction happen in a cultural context. Trying to understand its origin or treatment without considering the cultural context in which it occurs, will result in an inaccurate and partial understanding and treatment. For any recovery process to be effective, it needs to provide a recovery culture that offers at least the same level of meaning, brotherhood, and acceptance that the culture of addiction offered.

Fellowship

I believe that fellowship is the most curative aspect of 12-step programs. Most treatment professionals and addicts know that if an addict had the power to stop using on his/her own, they would. Ultimately, this is what distinguishes addicts from drug users: addicts are incapable of stopping on their own, while drug users can. All recovery processes offer a method for the addict to stop using. Hundreds of different methods have been used, but, unfortunately, most are unsuccessful. A common factor shared by most of the successful methods is some form of fellowship. To date, the most successful treatment for addiction is 12-step programs. What sets 12-step programs apart from the many other modes of treatment is that they are composed of very well-established and freely accessible socio-cultural networks. These cultural and social networks are the backbone of the Integrated Recovery approach. Without them, Integrated Recovery is jelly.

Nearly twenty years ago, I was a suicidal and hopelessly drug-hungry scavenger. I chose recovery not because I wanted to become a productive member of society or to contribute to the collective consciousness of the human race, but because I was lucky enough to be given the option of treatment. At the time it sounded like a better deal than sleeping hungry on a concrete floor in a "semi-perpetual" state of heroin withdrawal. And somehow, slowly, despite myself, I got better. I got better because I was loved for who I was at my lowest point. I had nothing to offer—but I was welcomed and accepted. The only intimacy I had known for a long time was the sharp, steely point of a hypodermic syringe. And somewhere along the way, I started feeling okay about myself and made a decision to give this "life-thing" a shot. Only because of the love and brotherhood I felt from those around me that shared the same predicament. All the theory, good intentions, maps, and so on are to no avail without love. We must remember, as recovering addicts or those helping addicts, that without a good measure of love and authentic connection, no recovery program will work in the long run. Social psychologist Erich Fromm goes as far to say that "love is the only sane and satisfactory answer to the problem of human existence."[156]

Scholars who support the "self-medication hypothesis" believe addicts often suffer from defects in their psychic structure due to poor relationships when they were young. This leaves them prone to external sources of gratification, i.e., drugs, sex, food, work, etc. in later life. Khantzian echoes this by saying that "substance abusers are predisposed to become dependent on drugs, because they suffer with psychiatric disturbances and painful effect states. Their distress and suffering is the consequence of defects in ego and self capacities which leave such people ill-equipped to regulate and modulate feelings, self-esteem, relationships, and behavior."[157] It is for this reason that the social recovery dimension is of utmost importance for an effective and sustainable recovery process. For addicts to develop a healthy and stable sense of self, they need to be in a supportive and knowledgeable social environment. The addict's psychic troubles were born from poor relationships and can only be modified via new relationships.

Self psychologists like Heinz Kohut believe that 12-step fellowships provide the ideal environment for addicts to heal their psychic deficits. Flores says "a person's denial of a need for others is also a denial of being human. It often leads us to substitute things (i.e., drugs, alcohol, sex, food) for human closeness, warmth, and caring. Historian Ernest Kurtz views the mutuality of AA—one alcoholic needing and helping another—as the cornerstone of the recovery process and the main reason why 12-step programs are so successful. Isolation of one's self from the rest of humanity is one consequence of shame and the driving force behind addiction, since the use of chemicals enhances the denial, fuels the grandiose defenses, and keeps one isolated."[158]

Twelve-step fellowships provide opportunity for supportive friendships, group participation, and mentoring. When actively participating in social fellowship activities like sponsoring, being sponsored, service, meetings, and informal fellowship activities, the individual starts to internalize these new healthy object-relations experienced within the fellowship. This results in a more stable, cohesive, and realistic sense of self and ways of relating to others, without which the recovering addict would continue to be plagued by feeling of emptiness, boredom, and poor relationships—which of course makes them more vulnerable to addictive behavior. William White states that often when addicts seek "to disengage from the culture of addiction, they find themselves alone, psychologically naked, and vulnerable. They realize that every person and place they know is connected to their drug use. Every thought and action is related to their drug relationship; their whole world is their drug relationship. As they seek to leave this world, they experience intense culture shock."[159] Addicts will find that their previous ways of dealing with the world no longer apply, and this cultural transition from the world of addiction to the world of recovery can be very daunting and overwhelming. He adds that for "recovery to occur, those physical, psychological, and social needs which were met in the culture must be addressed in different ways within new environments and relationships. The movement from addiction to recovery is a transformation in worlds and worldviews."[160] The social recovery dimension collectively refers to all relational, social, and cultural aspects of your Integrated Recovery Program.

The Culture of Recovery

To make the transition from the culture of addiction to the culture of recovery, we not only need to give up our old culture, but our needs and values must find expression within a new, supportive culture. It stands to reason that if addiction is an all-encompassing lifestyle, then to fill the void created by leaving the addiction lifestyle, recovery must become an equally all-encompassing lifestyle. One of the many reasons why 12-step meetings and fellowships are so successful is because of their capacity to fill the cultural void often found in the neophyte to recovery. White states that the "culture of recovery is an informal social network in which group norms (prescribed patterns of perceiving, thinking, feeling, and behaving) reinforce sobriety and long-term recovery from addiction. Like the culture of addiction, the culture of recovery is a way of life, a means of organizing daily existence, and a means of viewing people and events in the outside world. The culture of recovery constitutes an alternative career path for those who have been enmeshed in the culture of addiction.[161]

One component of an Integrated Recovery Program that is strongly suggested for the neophyte is 12-step meetings. Twelve-step meetings are the structure in which the cultural transformation takes place. Flores states, "[t]he chemically dependent individual responds more favorably to the group because the cultural and societal forces that contribute to addiction can be used in turn by the group to heal and treat the very deficit they have created."[162] Through meetings, the recovery neophyte learns a new way of life, makes friends, and gets the psycho-spiritual support that is crucial for his or her recovery. If you are new in recovery, meetings, or at least a supportive and informed social network, are an absolute necessity. Zoja echoes this by stating that when "placing together individuals who are all attempting to fight off their addiction, not only is community spirit instilled, but also an atmosphere of a mystical group which exalts and mutually reinforces their attempts at reaching a common goal."[163] He believes that this is a method relied upon by 12-step fellowships and is based on a hypothesis that "individual drug users are very prone to group phenomena. A group's code of behavior in the streets, for example the way its members acquire and take their drugs, seems to have not only a practical function but also a ritual one. Such behavior unconsciously recalls the ancient rites of entrance through which an individual was elevated into a more prestigious group of social class."[164]

From a social perspective, and in addition to 12-step fellowship meetings, 12-step culture provides social activities, fellowship conventions, and unofficial post-meeting get-togethers. All these social components of 12-step fellowships reinforce the cultural norms of recovery and deepen the connection with the fellowship. The number of 12-step meetings you attend, and the level of your participation in the fellowship, is dependent on your stage of recovery. If you are in early recovery, you will need more meetings than if you are twenty years clean. If you are ten years clean and attending seven meetings a week, then this may be an indication of an unbalanced life rather than working a good program. Some people erroneously equate the quality of recovery with the number of meetings they attend, and many use this as an excuse for unmanageability in other areas of their lives.

I don't think that addicts in recovery necessarily need to attend meetings for the rest of their lives. Some members of the fellowship hold a "fundamentalist" belief that old timers and members who stop attending meetings are sure to relapse. Apart from the fact that scores of people who eventually stopped going to meetings are still clean after a long period of time, this is a very dangerous, alienating, and ethnocentric belief, because it creates an "us against them" dichotomy. What does often cause people to relapse, however, is stopping all forms of psycho-spiritual work. But many who leave the fellowship simply join other fellowships and continue working on themselves by applying the principles they learned in the NA fellowship. Some join a spiritual community and find support there. If this is their choice, then we should respect that and wish them well. Do not think you are on the moral high ground just because you go to meetings and somebody else doesn't.

The Integrated Recovery approach makes suggestions but does not ostracize other recovering addicts for using a different approach. The dogma and methods are of secondary importance. What matters most is that addicts find a recovery process that works for them. Although the Integrated Recovery approach is informed by the 12-step program, I am not of the opinion that only 12-step fellowships can provide the necessary support for recovering addicts. There are many other social support systems. What I do believe is that some form of fellowship/social support is essential at the early stages of recovery—within 12-step culture or not.

Sponsorship

As with all heroic journeys, there is a mentor who motivates, guides, and teaches the hero or heroine along their quest. The famous mythologist Joseph Campbell says the following about the hero's journey: "We have not even to risk the adventure alone; for the heroes of all time have gone before us; the labyrinth is thoroughly known; we have only to follow the thread of the hero-path."[165] Mentors come in all forms and sizes, but the mentor always has something essential that the hero needs to successfully complete the journey. Twelve-step philosophies hold that recovery is only possible in the company and guidance of others. That is why each of the Twelve Steps starts with the pronoun "We." Apart from the guidance and knowledge that the sponsor or mentor provides for the recovery hero, the relationship in itself is profoundly healing. For many addicts, the relationship with their sponsor is their first healthy and intimate relationship with a human being. Through the relationship with a sponsor, the "interpersonal bridge" is restored.

As discussed earlier, a frequent cause of addiction is poor and dysfunctional early relationships. The relationship with a sponsor can serve as a healthy proto-relationship, and can reprogram past dysfunctional "object-relations." In the latest publication of the Narcotics Anonymous World Service, entitled *Sponsorship,* sponsorship is explained as follows: "Along with the Twelve Steps and Twelve Traditions, sponsorship is considered one of the cornerstones of the program and the NA way of recovery. The therapeutic value of one addict helping another is exemplified in this relationship with another NA member."[166] It is suggested that you find a sponsor of the same sex with more clean time than you. Look for somebody that has something you want and whom you respect.

Sponsorship and Men

Many men in recovery have distant or absent fathers. Some feel this is one of the contributing factors for addiction in men in contemporary post-industrial society. Many male addicts have never grown up and have never been initiated into manhood. A sponsor can function as the father a boy never had, guiding him gently but firmly into manhood. He can help him get in touch with his masculinity. Poet Robert Bly says that men who don't get in touch with their own masculinity often find themselves unable to make commitments and have healthy relationships. This is because they project their "souls" onto the woman they love. Bly referred to these men, in his book *Iron John,* as "Flying Boys."

Addiction and recovery have many rites of passage and often we need a mentor to authenticate these rites of passage. When a man does not grow up but remains a "Flying Boy," he will always be enmeshed with his mother and consequently develop an unhealthy feminine aspect in his psyche. Like in the 19th century fable of "Iron John," the mentor must help the young man steal the key from under the mother's pillow. A mother can never give "the key" to her son; it must be taken. Feminine energy tends to hold back, wants to bond, wants to enmesh. Masculine energy wants to differentiate, wants to be different. Without masculine influence, a man never learns to become his own being and can only exist with an enmeshed partner. Differentiation is experienced as death. Therefore, the young man needs a differentiated man to guide him from this "psychic death" to healthy manhood. He is then able to be in relation with the feminine without losing himself. The mentor/sponsor can also help the man deal with his "mother complex," a feminine archetype that can have disastrous consequences for a man.

Jungian analyst Robert Johnson writes that "[w]ithout any question, the mother complex is the most difficult encounter any man ever faces. It is the regressive capacity in him and will destroy his life more quietly than any other single element in his psychology. For a male to succumb to the mother complex is to lose the battle of life. The mother complex is his wish to regress to infancy again and to be taken care of, to crawl into bed and pull the covers over his head, to evade some responsibility that faces him."[167] Johnson continues, writing, "Nothing is as dangerous to a man as an unresolved mother complex. Skid row or a drug-and-alcohol rehabilitation center lies not far ahead for a man with a heavy mother complex."[168] A sponsor can help to resolve a mother complex in a sponsee. The mother complex in the context of addiction is an unhealthy dependence and projection of the feminine on another woman or outside object—the umbilical cord is still connected to his mother—and he unrealistically expects to be taken care of. The man has never learned to sever the cord from his mother and will always find himself in dependent relationships or with complexes. Much of sex and love addiction in men is an unhealthy and overly dependent relationship with the feminine.

A sponsor will help the neophyte male addict to internalize a healthy feminine—the capacity to self-soothe and self-regulate—and not be exclusively dependent on an outside source for these needs. The man with an un-severed umbilical cord will always be dependent for his "feminine needs" from the outside, and consequently his addiction will tend to migrate. His needs are always projected and always seeking comfort "out there." A sponsor can help the sponsee bring the relationship between the masculine and feminine parts of his psyche into balance. Erich Fromm says, "In this development from mother-centered to father-centered attachment, and their eventual synthesis, lies the basis for mental health and the achievement of maturity."[169]

Relationships

Earlier, I defined spirituality as "the quality of our relationships with ourselves, others, and our being-in-the-world." Relationships are an integral component of recovery. The quality of our interpersonal relationships is often an indication of how "well" our life is going. As Kohut suggests, "we are all object-seeking creatures from birth and the drive to form satisfying relationships is innate."[170] Recovery teaches us about healthy relationships and that healthy relationships are the source of our recovery.

In an Integrated Recovery Lifestyle, we aim to have healthy friendships, romantic relations, and family relations. Our recovery is intimately connected with our relationships; one cannot exist without the other. In the context of relationships, one of the major changes in recovery is when we move from a totally self-centered lifestyle to a lifestyle that includes and respects the needs of others. Systems and family theories have shown that our psycho-spiritual well-being must always be understood within the context of familial and social contexts. It is therefore of utmost importance in recovery that you choose your relationships wisely. There is a saying in NA, "Stick with the winners." If you associate with people with poor recovery, or those who do not respect your recovery, they will have a negative effect on your recovery lifestyle.

When married or in a romantic relationship, your recovery is greatly influenced by the quality of that relationship. I strongly recommend that you enter some form of therapy, ideally couples therapy, if struggling with any relationship issues. If you grew up in a dysfunctional family, chances are good that you internalized dysfunctional patterns of relating. These dysfunctional "object-relations" will likely present themselves in your romantic relationship. A good therapist will help you notice your dysfunctional patterns and provide alternative modes of being. For addicts who experienced sexual abuse in their past, long-term individual and couples therapy is often essential to be able to function in a healthy relationship.

Relationships can be understood as a composite of three interrelated and interdependent processes—we can use the analogy of a three-legged chair. One leg is your own process, the other leg your partner's process, and the last leg the relationship process. For a relationship to be effective, all three processes must be functional—if any of the legs break, the chair topples. I recommend the workbook for couples, *Open Hearts* by Patrick Carnes et al., if you are experiencing difficulties in a romantic relationship. *Open Hearts* is designed to be worked by the couple, together. Another good book is *How to be an Adult in Relationships: The Five Keys to Mindful Loving* by David Richo.

Service

Zen Buddhists take the Bodhisattva vow by saying, "Sentient beings are numberless; we vow to save them all." The belief that underlies this vow is that the Zen Buddhist will only opt for and become enlightened when all sentient beings have reached Nirvana. English poet John Donne echoes this: "Any man's death diminishes me, because I am involved in mankind; And therefore, never send to know for whom the bell tolls; It tolls for thee."[171] This seems like a very compassionate act, but it is based not only on selfless motives but also on an acceptance of reality.

If you grow developmentally from egocentric towards kosmocentric, then the higher up the developmental "ladder" you go, the more you realize and appreciate the true nature of your interrelatedness with all other sentient beings. Your happiness and their happiness become the same thing. Like a mother who cannot rest until her baby is satisfied, so as we become more aware, we realize our interconnectedness and that our well-being is forever tied to the well-being of all sentient beings. Therefore, the vow is not really an option but rather an ontological imperative. As Taoist philosopher Wei Wu Wei put it:

Why are you unhappy?

Because 99.9% of everything you think,

And everything you do,

Is for your self,

And there isn't one.[172]

Step Twelve states, "Having had a spiritual awakening as a result of these steps, we tried to carry this message to addicts and to practice these principles in all our affairs." Step Twelve is similar to the Bodhisattva vow; as we develop spiritually, we realize our interconnectedness with the fellowship and the world, and we realize that service is an integral part of further spiritual development. Service in 12-step fellowships has many obvious benefits: we make new friends, are given a sense of purpose, and are provided with an opportunity to forget our own life drama and problems. Service helps to contextualize our lives and our problems. Albert Einstein says, "A human being is part of the whole called by us universe, a part limited in time and space. He experiences himself, his thoughts and feelings as something separated from the rest, a kind of optical delusion of his consciousness. This delusion is a kind of prison for us, restricting us to our personal desires and affection for a few persons nearest to us. Our task must be to free ourselves from this prison by widening our circle of compassion to embrace all living creatures and the whole of nature in its beauty."[173]

Positive psychology states that the meaningful life in service of something bigger than us is the most powerful contributor to a truly happy life. His Holiness the 14th Dalai Lama said, "We are visitors on this planet. We are here for ninety years at the very most. During that period, we must try to do something good, something useful, with our lives. Try to be at peace with yourself, and help others share that peace. If you contribute to other people's happiness, you will find the true goal, the true meaning of life."[174] This sentiment is echoed by the authors of *Integral Life Practice*: "Service with a glad heart is a direct way to tap into the energy that sustains life and uplifts the spirit. It is truly in giving that we receive most fully. One of the core secrets of happy living is conscious practice of service with sincere intentionality."[175]

Seeing that the Integrated Recovery approach is an Integral approach, it does not limit service to ethnocentric fellowship alone but extends it to all sentient beings as well as the environment. From an Integrated Recovery perspective, any form of service is working Step Twelve—for example, joining Greenpeace, geopolitical service, conscious activism, charity work, or just being nice to somebody in need.

Designing the Social Recovery Dimension of Your IRP

You need the following components for your social recovery dimension to be sustainable:

- Fellowship
- A sponsor/mentor
- Service
- Relationships
- Social groups

The following suggestions and exercises will help you design and choose the appropriate practices to ensure that your social recovery dimension is functioning adequately.

1. Twelve-step Meetings: Are you attending 12-step meetings? How often? Are the number of meetings you attend appropriate for your stage of recovery? Do you have a home group?

2. Sponsor: Do you have a sponsor? How often do you meet or phone him or her? If your sponsor is not currently working for you, is there somebody else who can? Do you use your sponsor and do you follow his/her advice? If not, why?

3. Service: Are you doing service in the fellowship? What service? Is the service appropriate for your stage of recovery? What other forms of service are you doing for your community and environment? If you are new to recovery, remember that you must first serve yourself before you will be able to help others. Also remember that 12-step fellowships are not evangelical—they work on attraction rather than promotion.

4. Relationships: What is the quality of your current platonic relationships? Are you in a romantic relationship? How is it going? If you are experiencing trouble, have you considered therapy? If so, is your partner willing to engage in a therapeutic process? How are your familial relationships? If you have children, how is your relationship with them? Are you using your sponsor to help you with your relationship(s)? Remember, addiction is about our fear of intimacy and recovery is about taking the risk of intimacy.

5. Social groups: Are there any other groups or clubs you belong to? Joining groups or clubs in whatever form is a good way to expand your social world. Check the local paper and see what groups are available in your area. Join a band, meditation group, jogging or hiking club, spiritual discussion group, environmental activist organization—the list is endless.

CHAPTER 8
THE ENVIRONMENTAL RECOVERY DIMENSION

You can't make positive choices for the rest of
your life without an environment that makes
those choices easy, natural, and enjoyable.
~ Deepack Chopra

The great humanistic psychologist Abraham Maslow is well known for his theory of human motivation, in which he proposes that human motivation is determined by a hierarchy of needs.[176] He proposes there are at least five sets of basic needs: physiological, safety, love, esteem, and self-actualization. These five needs form a hierarchy, which orders our "urgency" to satisfy them—a hungry man with no home is not usually concerned with aesthetic or spiritual well-being until his physiological and safety needs are satisfied. Addiction exemplifies this theory. In many cases, our "addiction-needs" take precedence over other, higher needs. As discussed previously, because our addiction manifests as physiological and basic psychological needs, when they are not satisfied, all other needs take a back seat.

Maslow's theory of human motivation is important for an adequate understanding of your environmental recovery dimension. The environmental recovery dimension collectively refers to all the monetary, administrative, legal, and residential aspects of your Integrated Recovery Lifestyle. Using Maslow's model, we see that the previous five recovery dimensions we have discussed are related to the higher three needs (love, esteem, and self-actualization), whereas the environmental recovery dimension relates to the two lower needs, physiological and safety. Maslow would likely say that without your environmental recovery dimension taken care of, you will never be able to truly actualize the other five recovery dimensions. When you have serious financial, administrative, legal and/or residential problems, your more lofty goals of the Integrated Recovery Lifestyle are severely compromised.

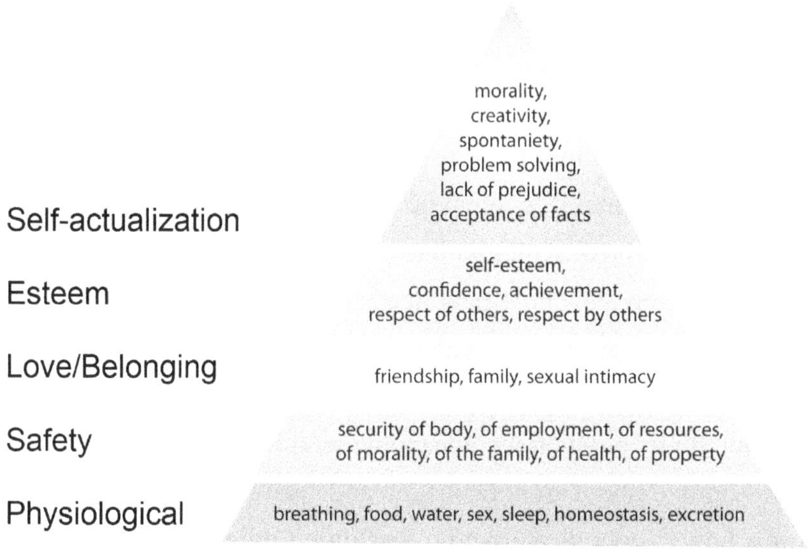

Self-actualization — morality, creativity, spontaniety, problem solving, lack of prejudice, acceptance of facts

Esteem — self-esteem, confidence, achievement, respect of others, respect by others

Love/Belonging — friendship, family, sexual intimacy

Safety — security of body, of employment, of resources, of morality, of the family, of health, of property

Physiological — breathing, food, water, sex, sleep, homeostasis, excretion

Figure 9: Maslow's Hierarchy of Needs

Traditionally, we might be in recovery and going to seven meetings a week, but be completely broke, in debt, with unmanageable lives, and still think our recovery is good, because we are "working a good program." The Integrated Recovery approach warns against and prevents such faulty thinking. If our financial, administrative, legal, and residential needs are unmanageable, then our whole program may come tumbling down. Although they "work a program," it is not uncommon for recovering addicts to relapse because of severe unmanageability in their financial recovery dimension. When our physiological and safety needs are not met, our higher needs become developmentally arrested, and the lower needs constantly take the foreground, thereby preventing higher needs from being actualized. It's like when you're watching a movie and towards the end you need to go to the loo; until this need is met, it is all you can think of and once satisfied, you can return to watch the film without distraction.

Fritz Perls highlights this point by stating that "the dominant need of the organism, at any time, becomes the foreground figure, and the other needs recede, at least temporarily, into the background... For the individual to satisfy his needs, to close the gestalt, to move on to other business, he must be able to sense what he needs and he must know how to manipulate himself and his environment, for even the purely psychological needs can only be satisfied through the interaction of the organism and the environment."[177]

Addicts, especially culturally-enmeshed addicts, are often profoundly inept when it comes to general life skills. Often we can philosophize about Schopenhauer and quantum physics, but not know how to operate a washing machine. Addicts in early recovery are easily overwhelmed by administrative issues that are second nature to most people. Many addicts' "administrative-intelligence" is very low in early recovery. It is advised therefore, that addicts in early recovery do not enter into work or financial situations that require a high degree of "administrative-intelligence," because this can create crippling anxiety and may consequently lead to relapse.

Monetary Responsibility

Most of us addicts in recovery, besides those with an overly co-dependent family, have to work for our money. Being financially secure is closely related to our feelings of safety. If we experience stress related to our financial well-being, then it will greatly influence our Integrated Recovery Lifestyle. Further, financial stability enables one to invest in therapies or practices that can enhance our program. Addicts often experience difficulties with finances—many tend to overspend or have trouble managing money. I recommend working out a budget; you can use your therapist or sponsor's assistance if needed. It may also be helpful to use the services of a financial adviser when dealing with complex financial issues. Many addicts enter recovery with debt, and a financial adviser can help to develop a repayment plan. Repaying our debt is one of the best ways to make amends.

The decision of what type of employment to pursue depends on your stage of recovery. If you are in early recovery, it is advised to get a low-stress job and not to worry too much about career and future. In the first year, your psychological health takes priority over job and career. If you build a solid foundation for your Integrated Recovery Lifestyle, then eventually it will translate into the capacity for financial security.

Administrative Manageability

We addicts tend to procrastinate, especially in the administrative area of our lives. We neglect our taxes, cars, bills, and chores. I believe we procrastinate so often for three reasons. The first is due to our emotional immaturity and egocentricity. We do not tolerate frustration well and often think we are "too cool for school." Due to this immature entitlement, we expect the world to have different rules for us. This is especially evident in administrative matters that demand a high threshold for frustration and require patience and perseverance. We need to learn to "live life on life's terms." A significant part of the recovery process for many recovering addicts is to learn how to do the boring chores of daily life.

The second reason we are prone to procrastinate is that because we are shame-based, we are constantly vigilant in situations that may expose us in all our "badness." Truly completing something exposes you and discloses your ability to yourself and the world. For shame-based people, anything short of perfection is experienced as not good enough and this activates our toxic shame. Through quitting and non-completion, we avoid this exposure and its positive potential.

The third reason is that many addicts have what Garret LoPorto, author of *The DaVinci Method*, calls the DaVinci personality, which is typical of those believed to have ADD/ADHD and "addictive personalities." One feature of the DaVinci personality is that they tend to think in wholes. LoPorto believes DaVincis tend to procrastinate and fail to complete things, because unconsciously they fear that completion of any project will result in their symbolic "death" (due to their always thinking of the big picture), and this creates huge anxiety. LoPorto says: "When you stop taking your self seriously, you will stop defending against your demise and in that relinquishment of defenses you will become intimately aware of the graceful impermanence of every aspect of life. This will liberate you to enjoy the moment and complete your goals without anxiety."[178]

Administrative tasks give us regular opportunities to change our pattern of procrastination and learn how to complete things—laying a new template—which makes it easier when we are faced with important projects. "As you progress through the agony of completion, experiencing the thrilling release of putting each incomplete project to rest, you will probably learn to only start what you intend to finish, because suffering through the completion of something you never really wanted is a most horrendous fate."[179] I have a simple rule: I am only allowed to change direction or give up on something once it is complete. If I am studying for an exam and I have an inclination to change my course or degree, I may do so only after completing the exam. If

I then still want to do so, I can. This simple rule protects me from impulsive decisions to quit, which are driven by unconscious fear, immaturity, or laziness. Managing your administrative affairs—paying taxes, servicing your car, cleaning your house, paying bills, having insurance, etc.—are important for a serene Integrated Recovery Lifestyle. You may meditate for ten hours a day, but if your administrative life is unmanageable, it will constantly create anxiety, affecting all other recovery dimensions.

Residential Security

It is a fact that the environment in which we live has a profound effect on our well-being. This is even more relevant for recovering addicts. This is because certain environments are conducive to recovery while others promote addiction. For each recovering addict, his "addiction-promoting" environment is unique. In the social recovery dimension, we explored the value of having a healthy social component to our recovery. All things social need infrastructure—addiction needs infrastructure and recovery needs infrastructure. As we move from the culture of addiction to the culture of recovery, we move from the infrastructure of addiction to the infrastructure of recovery. This is what NA means when it says to avoid "dangerous people, places, and things." Many addicts have relapsed and gone back to the culture of addiction, because they did not avoid the infrastructure of the addictive lifestyle.

If you live in an environment where there are no meetings and your housemates use and don't respect your recovery—then your environment is not beneficial to your recovery. In contrast, by living with individuals who support your recovery and in an environment where there is an active recovery community—then your environment is beneficial to your recovery. Obviously we all have certain financial and/or familial limitations and cannot always live where we want, but we must choose the best possible environment within our current limitations. As we grow in recovery our needs change, and consequently the type of environment that will be most suitable for us also changes.

We must also be aware of placing too much emphasis on our environment. In recovery circles this is often referred to as a "geographical"—when somebody moves in an attempt to fix personal issues. Most addicts have a long list of "geographicals" when they enter recovery. The problem is, wherever you go, there you are. It is always a good idea to consult those whom you trust when it comes to moving house or city. This is to ensure that you are doing the right thing for the right reasons, and this is particularly important for those in early recovery.

Designing the Environmental Recovery Dimension of Your IRP

The components you need to consider for optimal health in your environmental recovery dimension are:

- Work
- Monetary
- Residential
- Legal
- General administrative

The following suggestions and exercises will help you design and choose the appropriate practices to ensure that your

environmental recovery dimension is functioning adequately.

1. Work: What work are you currently doing? Is this appropriate for your current level of recovery? Is your working environment conducive to recovery? Is this the job you really want to do or is it a means to an end? What is your ideal job? Are you working towards your ideal job? Are you thinking of quitting your job? If so, have you consulted your therapist or sponsor?

2. Monetary: What is your current financial situation? If there is a problem, what do you think the problem is? Are you in debt? If so, by how much? What are your plans to repay debt? Do you need a financial advisor? What are your financial goals?

3. Residential: Are you happy where you are staying? Is your living environment conducive to recovery? If not, what are your plans to change this? Where and what is your ideal home? Are you working towards this ideal?

4. Legal: Do you have any legal problems? If so, are you getting the right help?

5. General administrative: In general, how is the administrative part of your life? Do you procrastinate with "boring" chores? Are there administrative components that are currently unmanageable? How does this affect your well-being? Are there administrative problems that are crippling other areas of your Integrated Recovery Lifestyle? Do you need

help from your therapist or sponsor to assist with your administrative issues? The simplest way to keep administration manageable is to keep a diary, list your priorities—and then do them. Remember every "boring" chore you do strengthens your capacity to complete projects in general—therefore every administrative task has a psycho-spiritual component.

CHAPTER 9
YOUR INTEGRATED RECOVERY PROGRAM

Whatever you can do, or dream you can,
begin it. Boldness has genius, power,
and magic in it. Begin it now!

~ Goethe

Now that we have come this far, you might think to yourself, what a tall order this recovery thing is. Yes, it is hard work—but it's no different from what anybody else is faced with who is trying to live a worthwhile life. We need only to do what we can, and we are allowed to make many mistakes along the way. If you put 50% of the effort you put into your addiction into your recovery, you will be just fine. This book has given you a detailed map of the recovery territory, as well as the nessesary tools, and now it is up to you to make the hero's journey, traveling alongside many other pilgrims. Each clean day in recovery holds its own boon.

There is the story of a young salesman who went to a farmer to sell him a book on farming. The salesman said, "This book tells you all you need to know about farming." The farmer replied, "Young man, that's not the problem. I know everything that is in that book. My problem is doing it."[180]

In the same way, this book will not mean much to you if you do not practice some of what's in it. When practicing all six recovery dimensions, each one will strengthen the other, and consequently we will heal and grow more rapidly than if we were only to practice one or two of these elements. Integrated Recovery is *"recovery cross-training."* This chapter will provide you with an overview of how to put together an Integrated Recovery Program (IRP). To assist you in developing an Integrated Recovery Lifestyle, I have created templates that can be used to design your Integrated Recovery Program and track your progress.[181] I will discuss each of the templates in the following sections of this chapter.[182]

Integrated Recovery Program Template

An Integrated Recovery Program template is a structure that you can use to design your IRP. There are two main components to an IRP: 1) the six recovery dimensions, and 2) the Integrated Recovery Graph.[183]

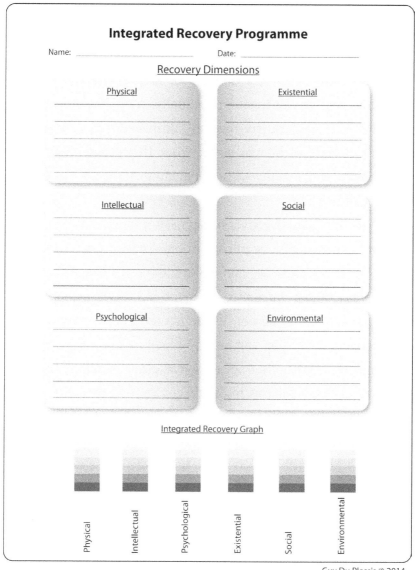

Figure 10: Template for the design of an
Integrated Recovery Program (IRP)

As discussed already, the six recovery dimensions are six different modes of your being-in-the-world that need to function sufficiently for a recovery program to be sustainable. Integrated Recovery theory states that none of these recovery dimensions can be left out and moreover, pathology in any one of them will compromise the whole system. Experience has shown us that when all of these recovery dimensions are healthy, our lifestyle is healthy, and we can function optimally. As indicated earlier in the book each of these six recovery dimensions also represents different clusters of human needs. Your IRP planner will assist you in identifying healthy ways of having these needs met in each recovery dimension.

The Integrated Recovery Graph (IRG) helps us to visually plot the developmental altitude of each of our six recovery dimensions. Therefore, at a glance, we and our sponsors or therapists can see which areas of our Integrated Recovery Lifestyle are optimally developed and which are not. We do not have to be exceptional in each recovery dimension, but rather optimal for our stage of overall development. Somebody with one year clean or ten years clean will have different focuses in their recovery, and their IRG's may look different, but one is not necessarily better "recovered" than the other—it is relative.

My aim, with the one-page template for the design of an IRP, was to find the simplest visual, conceptual system to adequately represent the complex recovery process, providing you with an accessible and easy-to-use "visual recovery structure." I designed this visual "map" to fit on one page, so you can stick it on your fridge or carry it in your wallet. You can fill in this template weekly or monthly or whenever the components of your program change. This provides you with clear goals and practices and will assist you in remaining accountable to yourself and/or your therapist/sponsor.

Before we move on to the second template, it will be useful to discuss the two types of development that happen in a recovery process and how this relates to the templates.

Horizontal and Vertical Development

According to Susanne Cook-Greuter, a leading adult developmental expert, human development can happen "vertically" and "horizontally." This is an important concept for us in recovery. It means that we can develop in two different but parallel ways. Cook-Greuter writes that "[l]ateral [or horizontal] growth and expansion happens through many channels, such as schooling, training, self-directed and life-long learning, as well as simply through exposure to life. Vertical [or stage] development in adults is much rarer. It refers to how we learn to see the world through new eyes, how we change our interpretations of experience, and how we transform our views of reality."[184]

We can therefore view and measure our recovery progress on two planes—the horizontal and the vertical (often referred to as translation and transformation in Integral Psychology). Our vertical growth in recovery was discussed in the chapter on Integral Theory and refers to the egocentric, ethnocentric, and worldcentric stages of development, and the different stages of recovery. As we slowly and painstakingly grow through these levels, our perspective of ourselves and the world changes; it gradually becomes less self-centered and more inclusive and embracing.

We use the IRG to indicate our vertical development in each of our recovery dimensions. As we have seen, each of our six recovery dimensions can also be at different stages of vertical development. Your IRG helps you to see which of your recovery dimensions are functioning at adequate, or less than adequate, levels. As stated before, we need not excel in each of these recovery dimensions unless we choose to, but, minimally, we need to function at a reasonable level of health in all of them for our overall development to be healthy. For the sake of simplicity, the IRG plots three stages: pathological, adequate, and excellent. These correlate with the pre-conventional, conventional, and post-conventional levels of development, as articulated by developmental scientists and Integral theorists.

The Integrated Recovery Wheel

The horizontal or lateral growth of your Integrated Recovery Lifestyle is a measure used to judge how well you have practiced each of your recovery dimensions within a chosen time frame, which could be daily, weekly, or even monthly. The scales used for horizontal growth do not correlate with stages of development but can be compared with a test or assessment of a practice, as in, "How much of what you should have done did you do?" The idea is that constant horizontal practice (or translation) in a recovery dimension will translate into vertical development (or transformation) in that recovery dimension, and eventually contribute to overall vertical development.

I use a hexagonal-circular model called the Integrated Recovery Wheel (IRW) to illustrate our Integrated Recovery Lifestyle on a horizontal plane and within a chosen time frame. The inner circle signals dangerous behaviors or risk factors, and the outer circle signifies the healthy practices or protective factors that are taking place in your six recovery dimensions within a specific time frame. From a needs perspective, the outside circle represents healthy ways of having your needs met, which actually authentically satisfy the needs. Whereas, the inner circle represents unhealthy attempts of having your needs met—what Chilean economist Max-Neef calls "pseudo-satisfiers." These pseudo-satisfiers are attempts of having a need met "that generate a false sense of satisfaction of a given need."[185]

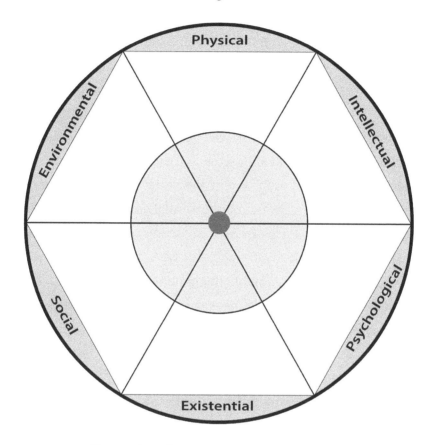

Figure 11: The Integrated Recovery Wheel[186]

Our vertical development does not fluctuate on a daily or weekly basis and takes considerable time to progress or regress. On the other hand, horizontal growth in each of our six recovery dimensions can fluctuate dramatically. For example, on Monday, you ate well, jogged, and went surfing. Therefore your physical recovery dimension scores high for that day. Then, on Tuesday, you ate five Big Macs, watched TV the whole day, and consequently, your physical recovery dimension scores low. So Monday you score high but on Tuesday not. Neither will affect your vertical physical recovery dimension, but long-lasting patterns will.

The IRW is used in the form of a daily diary, where, for each of the six recovery dimensions, healthy recovery actions (protective factors) are indicated in the outer circle and dangerous behaviors (risk factors) are indicated in the center. Each day, you can also score yourself (from 0 to 10) for each of your recovery dimensions. This provides you with a total daily score when added together as well as a weekly score for each recovery dimension when the scores for each day in the week are totaled. For the purpose of keeping score of your horizontal development, you can use various indices. Each of your daily scores can be recorded on a Weekly Integrated Recovery Index for each week and then over a period of a month on a Monthly Integrated Recovery Index. These enable you to see patterns in the way you practice your Integrated Recovery Program. If you continue—on average—to score well in each of your recovery dimensions, this will translate into vertical development and reduce the likelihood of relapse. We either work on our recovery or on our relapse. Both are a process.

Monthly Integrated Recovery Index							Total:
	Week1	Week 2	Week 3	Week 4	Week 5		
Phys							
Intel							
Psych							
Exis							
Soc							
Env							

Weekly Integrated Recovery Index								Total:
	Mon	Tues	Wed	Thurs	Fri	Sat	Sun	
Phys								
Intel								
Psych								
Exis								
Soc								
Env								
							Total:	

Figure 12: Integrated Recovery Indices[187]

Relapse Prevention

John Dupuy often points out that relapse starts as soon as we stop working a recovery program. I agree completely. As addicts, addiction is our natural state; our body-mind has become conditioned to perpetuate this state of being. If we do not oppose the negative forces of addiction, it will continue automatically. A recovery program is about counteracting our natural automatic inclination to revert back to our addictive condition. Common sense would say that if you stay clean long enough, you will be completely healed from this affliction, and all reminiscences of its existence will disappear, like with many other diseases. There are two primary reasons why this is not the case.

First, addiction significantly rewires the "reward pathways system" of the brain, and regardless of clean time, these dysfunctional neuronal patterns remain to some extent. Therefore, even with twenty years clean, your brain still may have the same addictive potential it had twenty years before. Hence the statement in NA, "We pick up where we left off." This means that when you use again, your addiction often continues from the point you were at when you stopped. There are seldom any honeymoon periods or controlled using, but rather, *BANG*—straight back to major unmanageability and powerlessness.

The second reason is that addiction has many potential causes. You became an addict for a reason. If you remain abstinent without working a program, these causal factors will continue to make you prone to addiction. And, even if you mange to stop your primary addiction without treating the underlying conditions, your addictive patterns will likely migrate to other types of addictive behavior. Working an effective recovery program addresses your addiction's underlying causes and, once healed, will free you from the need to engage in addictive behavior. Nevertheless, you still carry the physiological and psychological potential for addiction and can relapse if you engage in addictive behavior.

Relapse can only happen when our consciousness narrows or collapses. A craving, by nature, is a momentary narrowing of our awareness. If, when we are caught in a craving, we forget past damages and future consequences and focus on the immediate rush—we are aware of only a fragment of our existence. In this condition of narrow awareness, using always seems like a good idea. I sometimes refer to this narrowing of consciousness as the "worm's eye view," as opposed to the "bird's eye view," which is a more comprehensive and inclusive view of our reality. As soon as our awareness expands and we adopt a "bird's eye view," aspects of our past and future enter our consciousness, and suddenly using does not seem that appealing anymore. In this context, we see why meditation and mindfulness practice is helpful, as they expand our awareness—which counteracts cravings and irrational thinking. One of the best and easiest ways to overcome a craving is to "come to your senses"—get out of your head and focus your awareness on any sensory experience: taste, smell, sight, touch, sounds—which automatically and almost instantaneously expands your awareness, consequently counteracting the craving. In fact, this simple technique works for any negative mental-emotional experience.

The IRW can also be used as a relapse prevention awareness tool. In the middle circle, you can indicate which behaviors can be dangerous for you or make you prone to relapse in each of the six recovery dimensions. For instance, in the physical dimension, it might be when you eat poorly and get no exercise. In the social recovery dimension, it might be socializing with your old using buddies. Relapse is a process, and there are often signs, which indicate that your recovery program is not functioning optimally and you are gravitating towards relapse. Indicating what these behaviors are for each of your six recovery dimensions on the IRW will provide you with cognitive insight as to when you are in danger. When you spot any of these middle circle behaviors, a red warning light should go on for you. For instance, when my house and surroundings become shoddy, it is normally a sign that there is something wrong—a red light goes on, and I know I need to look into what it is that is not optimal in my recovery system.

Recovery and relapse can be viewed as two poles of a continuum. We are always somewhere on the "relapse-recovery continuum," moving back and forth. The closer we get to the relapse pole, the more danger we are in; the closer we are to the recovery pole, the safer we are from possible relapse and the healthier our lifestyle. It is beyond the scope of this book to provide an adequate discussion of relapse prevention. I suggest that you consult one of the many books on the topic and work with your sponsor or therapist on specific tools that fit your circumstances. It is important that you understand what your personal triggers are, and that you develop effective tools to handle these situations.

Stop Technique

The STOP technique is a relapse prevention tool and awareness training method I developed. The acronym **STOP**, stands for **S**top, **T**ake a breath, **O**bserve, and **P**roceed. This simple exercise helps you become aware of your current situation and respond consciously instead of reacting automatically.[188]

The STOP technique can be applied in any situation and will, in most instances, increase awareness of your inner and outer worlds and enhance the affectivity of any decision or action consequently taken. What makes this method so effective is its simplicity and brevity. The STOP technique is comprised of four steps.

> ➤ The first step is, when faced with any difficult or stressful situation, simply stop or slow down all action and/or train of thought to the best of your ability.

➤ The second step is to take a breath and "come to your senses." Focus only on your breathing, touch, or smell, or any other sense. This mindful exercise will immediately expand your awareness and create a more objective perspective on your current situation.

➤ The third step is to observe your current situation by using the six recovery dimensions as a guiding structure. Explore what is happening in the here and now for you physically, intellectually, psychologically, existentially, socially, and environmentally. Do not judge and analyze your situation; merely describe and label your perception non-judgmentally. This non-judgmental labeling of your current situation in a holistic fashion will once again increase your awareness of your perceived reality. In this step, you could observe how your current thoughts are influencing your feelings and perception.

➤ The final step is to make a decision, based on your new-found awareness of your current situation, about how to proceed in relation to your thoughts, attitude, and behavior. From a 12-step perspective, this final step can be understood as a Step Three action—a conscious alignment with your own moral and recovery code.

The STOP technique can be used in virtually any situation and is particularly useful for addicts as a relapse prevention tool. When craving or when in, or assessing, a possible high risk situation, the application of this tool is very powerful.

High Altitude Recovery

The Integrated Recovery approach is also very useful for individuals with many years in recovery. Traditional recovery literature and theory mostly focus on early recovery and are usually pathological and problem-oriented, providing guidance for how to get out of trouble. Very little is written about high altitude recovery—for those in long term recovery who are doing really well and who are not "just-one-drink-away."

Many recovering addicts in higher altitude recovery leave recovery communities because their needs are no longer met. This is very unfortunate. The Integrated Recovery approach offers a medium for those at high recovery altitudes who still want to be part of a recovery community. An unfortunate misunderstanding exists in some recovery fellowships, when people who express their special and different needs are seen as heretics. This attitude is appropriate for the newcomer in order to keep his or her special-and-different, narcissistic–impulsive tendencies to being "terminally hip and fatally cool" in check. It is an appropriate attitude for the recovery neophyte at pre-conventional, egocentric stages of development. But this attitude is not appropriate for the "old timers" who obviously have different, and often more complex, needs compared to the newcomer. Intolerance towards anything that resembles individualism is a gross misunderstanding of the pluralistic 12-step philosophy and has unfortunate consequences. A healthy fellowship needs to hold the sameness and uniqueness of its members wherever they are developmentally.

A drawback of not viewing the recovery journey from a developmental perspective is thinking that recovery is about reaching the "recovery nirvana," often referred to as "serenity" in 12-step fellowships. This is not to say that recovering addicts don't get more serene, but rather that there is no final place of "ultimate serenity." Developmental theories enlighten us to the fact that each new stage brings forth its own rewards, challenges, and possible pathologies. Moreover, each new stage requires more sophisticated "recovery technology" to be able to navigate the new stage appropriately. As I've said before, the recovery program that worked for you when you were two years clean will not necessarily hold water when you are ten years clean. Also, the problems you now face are likely to be more complex and need more complex solutions and practices. Recovery does not usually get easier (in the context of practice), it actually gets more complex and difficult as we evolve. And if you are not equipped to deal with the new challenges of the stage you are entering, you will most likely find yourself miserable and disillusioned with the whole process. A common form of advice for "old timers" when faced with "developmental problems" of high altitude recovery is "to go back to basics." This type of advice does not always work and in some cases may be counterproductive.

So, the recovery program you practiced when you were a year clean may not be what you need now. You need to include and transcend the paradigm or practices of the previous stage—include your previous practices but also add to them. I have seen many recovering addicts over ten years clean, who seem perplexed by their recovery process; they are working their program diligently, but not feeling as good as they once did in early recovery. If we look at this phenomenon from a developmental perspective, it is obvious why: the recovery practices that worked at a previous stage will not be effective at a new stage. They may still have many benefits, but they need to be augmented to be effective at the higher recovery stage.

As pointed out before in our discussion on stages of development, a developmental map of recovery can be very useful, especially for those at higher stages of recovery. Clinical social worker and researcher Gary Nixon suggests that the recovery process can be understood in three stages, similar to my addiction/recovery stage model discussed in the section on stages of development. In stage one, the focus is on abstinence from alcohol and drugs. This stage correlates with what I refer to as early stage recovery. In stage two, similar to my middle stage recovery, the "behavioral abstinence of stage one recovery can be enhanced by working through a range of prepersonal and personal emotional issues of stage two recovery, such as dissolving the false core driver and reestablishing basic trust, reintegrating the shadow, dismantling the internal critic, burning though social anxiety and co-dependency patterns, dismantling the crystallized ego, and embracing existential issues of meaning and authenticity."[189] In stage three, which I call the transpersonal stage of recovery, Nixon applies Wilber's ego-transcendence transpersonal levels, and states that "clients learn to let go of their separate self egos in each moment to embrace nondual living and become fully integrated beings. The long journey of transformation turns from the initial descent of addiction to a wondrous beingness of moment to moment existence for the person who has now fully embraced stage three recovery."[190] In my addiction/recovery developmental model, as pointed out before, I include a level of development referred to as high altitude stage recovery between Nixon's stage two and stage three recovery.

What Nixon refers to as stage one and stage two recovery, and I call early and middle stage recovery, is fairly well articulated in recovery literature, and there is significant guidance for those at these stages. On the other hand, there is very little guidance for those who are at a high altitude stage or for those at a stage three/transpersonal stage of recovery. At a high altitude stage and at a stage three/transpersonal stage of recovery, it now becomes the recovering addict's responsibility to seek guidance beyond the confines of traditional recovery literature and fellowship. There are many communities and teachers that can assist in these stages of development. The Integral community is one such example. It is encouraging to see, for many recovering addicts entering these stages of development, that there is recovery literature emerging that is beginning to address these higher stages of recovery.[191]

Progress not Perfection...

One of the perils of any personal development program is that we can develop unrealistic expectations of ourselves and our development. Unrealistic expectations force us to continuously measure ourselves against unattainable and perfectionist ideals. Instead of improving our well-being, this adds to our distress and feelings of inadequacy. As addicts working any recovery program, we run the risk of succumbing to this inherent problem. Addicts are known to have perfectionistic tendencies with over-developed inner critics, fueled by low self-esteem. Our low self-esteem often drives us relentlessly to prove to others and ourselves that we are okay. If our perfectionism gets out of hand, we may always feel like our recovery lifestyle is not good enough, and we may continuously compare ourselves with others who appear to be doing better.

The Voice Dialogue theory of Hal and Sidra Stone can illustrate how we fall prey to being driven relentlessly by perfectionist standards. They believe that we have many "voices," or energy patterns, that make up our personalities. They warn of the danger when our "pusher" and "critic" voices operate outside our awareness and drive us relentlessly, always making us believe that whatever effort we make is not good enough. They say that the "birth of personality is coincident with the birth of this consciousness—the protector/controller energy patterns. The protector/controller observes our environment and determines which of our behaviors will work best and please the most people... As we mature, the protector/controller functions increasingly as a master computer network. It utilizes some of our other selves— our primary selves—to accomplish its ends. These selves define us and how we will behave and interact.[192]

Our primary selves are the voices or energy patterns that our controller/pusher employs to ensure our survival. Our primary voices are also the energy patterns we identify most strongly with. In our contemporary, competitive culture, many of us tend to primarily identify with our pusher, inner critic, perfectionist, and pleaser voices. When these voices function without an "aware ego," and we become solely identified with any of these voices at any given time, we then believe what they "say" is true. We believe that we are not good enough, not working hard enough, not living up to our potential, etc. These voices are not bad or wrong, but become problematic when any of them takes over our psyche in the absence of an "aware ego." As a result, we become completely identified with the voice or energy pattern without the guidance of our other voices, or an "aware ego." The idea is not to suppress or exorcise any of these voices. We need our pusher voice, or we will never do anything about our lives. We need the critic voice to guide us when we are wrong. But with a functioning "aware ego," they are merely part of a host of voices. Our "aware ego" takes guidance from all of them in order to decide on the best course of action.

Our primary voices or energy patterns, in their pathological versions, correlate with what Stanley Block refers to as the "Fixer." We need these voices to drive us. Our survival depends on them, but when we start "fixing" what isn't broken, then it becomes problematic. If we try to "fix" our mistaken belief of a "broken, shame-based core" by working a program, it may add to our existing shame. Instead, a recovery program is to be worked so that we get closer to realizing that we can never be broken at our core and that we are good enough as we are now, even with all of our so-called "defects."

Block's work further illustrates the "shadow" or potential pitfalls of working a recovery program. Central to Block's theory of the human personality is what he calls the human Identity System, or I-System. He states that the "human Identity System evolved in order to confirm and deepen the separateness of family, clan, religion, culture, race, nation, and species—i.e., to help us create our individuality. Without it, humans would lack self-interest, direction, and drive."[193] It becomes problematic when our I-System becomes overactive, thereby exaggerating our sense of separateness by restricting awareness. Our I-System has two sets of voices whose purpose is to reinforce its core beliefs, known as the "Fixer" and the "Depressor." Furthermore, our I-System has requirements about ourselves, others, and the world. When these requirements are not met, the Fixer and the Depressor are activated. The Depressor is our negative self-talk, always putting us down, often internalized from our parents. The fixer voice, often encouraged by therapy and coaching, is the voice that motivates us to action—in an unconscious attempt to "fix ourselves." The problem is that any action driven by the Fixer, achieved or not, has the Depressor waiting in its shadows.

Let's look at an example. Your Fixer tells you to get a degree; the belief is that once you have a degree, you will feel good about yourself. You study for years and get the degree, for a while you feel good, and then the feeling fades and your Depressor may start saying things like, "Everyone has a degree. It is nothing special, and you did not even get a distinction." Then your Fixer may come to the rescue and suggest you get a PhD, because then you will *really* be okay, and so the cycle starts again. Sound familiar? Now there is nothing wrong with getting a degree when it is something you want to do as a result of, what Block calls, your natural functioning. If we operate from our natural functioning, the aim is to not fix anything, but about enjoying it or taking care of it out of practical necessity.

Block advocates Mind-Body Bridging techniques to free us from the clutches of the I-System so that we can function naturally. "Mind-Body Bridging regulates what brain researchers call *Default Mode Network* and activates the *Executive Network*, which is the healthiest and most productive brain functioning. When the *Executive Network* is active, our mind and body heal as efficiently and quickly as possible, and we experience our inner Source of healing, goodness, power, and wisdom. We call this natural functioning. In a state of natural functioning, we feel connected to ourselves, others, the environment, and our inner Source of wellness."[194]

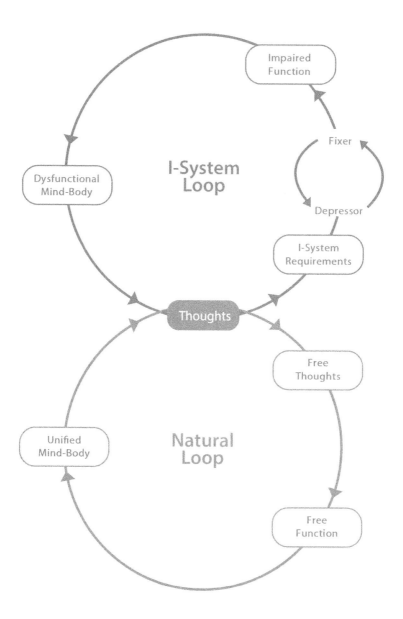

Figure 13: The I-System Loop and the Natural Loop[195]

In the above diagram, Block explains that the Natural Loop represents our natural state, where our thoughts generate free functioning and a unified body-mind state. The I-System Loop illustrates that whenever events or thoughts violate requirements, the I-System Loop is activated. The Depressor/Fixer cycle creates anxiety, body tension, and contracted awareness. The resulting impaired functioning creates a dysfunctional body-mind state in which we experience ourselves as a "Damaged Self." Each step in the I-System Loop reinforces the other steps to create a vicious cycle. Mind-Body Bridging practices return us to the Natural Loop.[196]

What follows are some Mind-Body Bridging practices suggested by Block. You may see correlations between some of these Mind-Body Bridging practices and the mindfulness practices already discussed so far in this book.

- By briefly and frequently returning to Background Sounds, we will nourish our body, mind, and spirit and will prevent the Damaged Self from running our life.

- Tuning into Body Sensations is crucial in allowing us to use the body-mind as a compass in our life. The I-System causes us to become numb to our body. We miss the vital signs of body tension and organ dysfunction. We don't need to do anything with the sensations, just include them in our expanded field of awareness.

- How many things have you touched today and been unaware of what it felt like? How many times today have you been aware of our constant companion, gravity? Sensing Touch and being Aware of Gravity is a powerful practice.

- Labeling Thoughts (e.g., "I'm having the thought that no one loves me") prevents our I-System from creating a dysfunctional body-mind state (Damaged Self). The I-System wants us to believe we are only as good as our last thought.

- Any time your Storyline (pet peeves or favorite Daily Drama) appears in thought or conversations, just be aware that your sequence of thoughts is bulking up your I-System and masking over your true self. Simply be aware and turn your attention to what you are presently doing.

- By shining our light of awareness upon our negative self-talk, we Befriend the Depressor. Our natural negative thoughts will always be there, but if the I-System doesn't capture them, they will soon fade. The bottom line is not about negative or positive thoughts but about always functioning freely in our natural loop.

- Befriending the Fixer is a little more subtle than our work with the Depressor. With practice, we will be able to differentiate natural functioning, which takes care of us and our responsibilities, from the tension-filled, driven, repetitive Fixer activity. By shining our light of awareness, we can shift from Fixer to natural functioning.[197]

- Recognizing and Defusing Requirements are key to remaining in your natural loop.

Block states that, "Resting the I-System by only using the Bridging Awareness Practices does not change the counter-productive nature of the I-System. For a Mind-Body Bridging intervention to be complete and effective, the I-System must be befriended and transformed by Defusing Requirements".[198] According to Block, "Requirements" are the beliefs we have of how we, others, and the world should be. In 12-step culture, it is well known that unrealistic expectations eventually lead to resentments – and resentments may lead to relapse. Consequently, a central feature of working a 12-step program is letting go of many of our "cherished" expectations.

It is essential that we try our best to work our recovery programs from our natural functioning and not solely driven by our Fixer. If your recovery is driven by your Fixer, you will most likely be plagued by feelings of inadequacy due to a never-ending striving towards unrealistic and perfectionistic standards. You will immediately feel when any activity is driven by your Fixer, as there will be a disproportionate level of anxiety present. When an activity is driven by our natural functioning, we are not that attached to the outcome and can enjoy the process in the here-and-now, regardless of the results.[199]

Being-in-Recovery vs. Doing-in-Recovery

Throughout most of this book, we have focused primarily on the "doing" of recovery, the how and why of the various practices of a recovery lifestyle. Another equally important, and perhaps even more important component of recovery, is what I call the "modes of being-in-recovery." What I mean by this term is that for every recovery practice we do, there is an attitudinal, or being, component, which is the way we relate to the practice. These modes of being-in-recovery can either be authentic or inauthentic; they either create an "openness" or "closed-ness" in our being-in-the-world.

Philosophers of existence like Martin Heidegger have pointed out that our modern society places an over-emphasis on doing (agency gone awry) and often neglects being. We are relentlessly driven by our goals and equate our happiness with what we achieve. We neglect the part of our inner self that values the quality of experience and the quality of relationships. Even though many people have recently changed their focus from materialistic goals to so-called spiritual goals, through practices like yoga or meditation, they are often still driven by a need for achievement and a goal-directed attitude. Now, instead of being driven relentlessly towards a materialistic endgame, they are driven relentlessly towards a spiritual endgame. The consequences to the self will be the same, as it is not only the results (whether material or spiritual) that lead to an authentic existence and inner content. What ultimately matters is our relationship and attitude towards these goals, and our experience of pursuing these goals.

In the context of recovery, there is a similar danger when we pursue our recovery goals without paying attention to our relationship with these goals and our recovery practices. The practice, or doing-in-recovery, should not be confused with being-in-recovery, in the same way that learning to play an instrument should not be confused with the joy of just playing the instrument. Very often, those of us who are involved in a process of self-development or a recovery program spend so much time practicing and "self-developing" that we forget to live—we forget to enjoy our mere being and our being-with-others.

So what are these modes of being-in-recovery, and paradoxically, how do we practice or achieve them? These attitudinal or being components can correlate with the spiritual principles of the Twelve Step program, the character strengths of positive psychology, and the principles of mindfulness as outlined earlier in this book. For example, you can participate in a 12-step meeting with an open attitude of humility, gratitude, and willingness, or with an attitude of arrogance and closed-mindedness. The attitude of your participation will profoundly affect the value you get from the practice. I call these attitudinal or modes of being-in-recovery our "existential attitude" towards a practice. In short, each recovery practice can be understood as having two qualities: the doing, or the result of the practice, and the being, or existential attitude towards the practice. Each of our recovery dimensions can consist of healthy practices which are done to the utmost, but if they are done with an inauthentic existential attitude, it will seriously compromise or could even have a destructive effect on our well-being. For example, you could be going to the gym five times a week, but if this is mediated by inauthentic existential attitudes, like perfectionism and over-criticalness, driven by your fixer and pusher, it could lead to a negative influence on you recovery and result in less freedom and suffering, rather than more openness and serenity.

Therefore, an essential element when working a program, and I cannot stress this enough, is that we need to pay attention to our existential attitude towards all of the components of our practice. I would go so far to say that the overall quality of our recovery is determined by the quality of our existential attitudes, rather than the results and quantity of our practices. In practical terms, this means that when we design our program and participate in our practices and relationships, we focus and remain mindful of our existential attitudes. Therefore, when doing our daily diaries, exploring or discussing our practices with a sponsor or therapist, we need to articulate and evaluate our existential attitudes towards our multitude of practices and our being-in-the-world. Practice alone is not enough; only a recovery program that incorporates authentic existential attitudes will be sustainable in the long run. It is important that you find a healthy balance between "doing" and "being," and that your recovery program does not become another futile attempt to "fix what ain't broke."

Your recovery practice is a paradox. You have to work hard, very hard in fact—not to fix yourself—but to realize that essentially you are good enough as you are right now, and that you have always been good enough. Simply put, the aim of working a recovery program is not about fixing yourself, but rather a process of awakening to the fact that there is nothing to fix..

Designing your IRP

For the final exercise of this book, I want you to fill in your Integrated Recovery Program Planner and then answer the following questions. Fill it in relative to where you are right now in your recovery. On your Integrated Recovery Graph, indicate where you feel you are developmentally in each of your recovery dimensions. This will highlight areas where you might need to work harder. Whenever you are faced with major life changes, re-evaluate your Integrated Recovery Program, as new situations and new levels of development require a different emphasis in each of your recovery dimensions. All the templates used in this book can be downloaded from my website www.guyduplessis.com.

1. In which of the recovery dimensions are you doing the best? Which are your weaker recovery dimensions? Are any of your recovery dimensions in a pathological

egocentric stage? Are there any of your recovery dimensions in which you are doing poorly or below average? If so, what practices are you not doing, or what factors are causing this? And what do you intend to do about it? What help is available for you in these areas?

2. Do you feel your overall center of gravity is optimal for your clean time? If not, what are the practices and recovery dimensions that need attention? Are the various practices of your recovery dimensions appropriate for your stage of recovery? Are you overcompensating in some of your recovery dimensions?

3. Do you have realistic expectations for your Integrated Recovery Program? Are you pushing yourself too much in any area? If so, which recovery dimension(s)? Have you spoken to your sponsor or therapist about your unrealistic expectations?

4. Find a quiet place and imagine your Integrated Recovery Lifestyle in five years time. Give yourself complete creative license and imagine the most ideal Integrated Recovery Lifestyle. Visualize this as clearly as you can and then write it down or draw it or make a collage. If you want, frame it, or stick it on your fridge. Put it where you can see it until it is internalized. Although there is no final destination, we all need goals and dreams in our lives. Integrated Recovery is about

unfolding your potential to provide the opportunity to work towards your dreams.

5. Relapse Prevention: Fill in your Integrated Recovery Wheel from the perspective of relapse prevention. In the middle circle, for each recovery dimension, write down your behaviors that indicate poor recovery or dangerous conduct. Be as specific as you can. Circle the behaviors that you are currently displaying. In the outside circle write all of your recovery practices for each recovery dimension. Make two lists of your middle circle behaviors: one that is indicative of poor recovery or potential relapse, but that you are not currently displaying, and the other of all the behaviors that are currently active. For each of the points, write down practices or tools that can counteract these particular behaviors or attitudes. For all your current "relapse behaviors," write down your plan of action. Draw a straight line which represents your "Relapse-Recovery Continuum". Indicate where you think you are on this continuum. Are you happy with where you are? If not, what are you going to do about it?

6. Integrated Recovery Wheel: You can now use your IRW on a daily basis as an extension of you daily diary, or on a weekly or even a monthly basis to keep track of how you are practicing your Integrated Recovery Lifestyle. If you are new to recovery or this approach, it is advised that you use the IRW daily until you get the hang of it. For each day, you can indicate—

using a number system from 0-10—how you did in each recovery dimension. Remember, progress not perfection.

7. Recovery Indices: For the next month, use a WRI and a MRI to keep score of how you practiced your IRP. You can use a score from 0 to 10 for each day of a recovery dimension, indicating at what level you worked your recovery dimension that day. Remember, it is all relative to what you initially planned for your personalized Integrated Recovery Program.

8. As indicated in this chapter, your "existential attitude" towards your various recovery practices is an essential component of a balanced recovery program. Write down and explore your existential attitude towards each aspect of your recovery program in the six recovery dimensions. Explore in which areas you have inauthentic existential attitudes, and with what authentic existential attitudes these can be replaced (see the spiritual principles of the Twelve Steps, character strengths of positive psychology, and mindfulness principles). Remember that your existential attitude towards anything is your choice, and can be changed any time you choose.

REFERENCES:

Alberts, S. (2012). *Eating Mindfully: How to End Mindless Eating & Enjoy a Balanced Relationship with Food.* Oakland, CA: New Harbinger Publications, Inc.

Alcoholics Anonymous. (1976). *Alcoholics Anonymous Big Book* (3rd Ed). New York: AA World Services, Inc.

Alcoholics Anonymous. (1987). *Twelve Steps and Twelve Traditions*. New York: AA World Services, Inc.

Abrahamson, A. E. & Pezet, A. W. (1976). *Body, Mind, and Sugar*. New York: Pyramid Books.

Alexander C., Robinson P., Rainforth M. (1994). Treating and preventing alcohol, nicotine, and drug abuse through transcendental meditation: a review and statistical meta-analysis. *Alcoholism Treatment Quarterly*.11 (1/2), 13–87.

Alexander, B.K. (2008). *The Globalization of Addiction: A Study in Poverty of the Spirit*. Oxford: Oxford University Press.

Alexander, B. K. (2010). A Change of Venue for Addiction. Retrieved July 11 from *http://globalizationofaddiction.ca/ articles-speeches/dislocation-theory-addiction/250-change-of- venue.html.*

Alexander, C., Druker, S. & Langer, E. (1990). Introduction: Major issues in the exploration of adult growth. In C. Alexander & E. Langer (Eds.). *Higher Stages of Human Development,* pp. 3-32. New York: Oxford University Press.

American Psychiatric Association (1994). *Diagnostic & Statistical Manual of Mental Disorders* (4th ed.). Washington, DC: APA.

Amodia, D.S., Cano, C. & Eliason, M.J. (2005). An integral approach to substance abuse. *Journal of Psychoactive Drugs*, 37 (4), 363-371.

Baer, R. A., Mindfulness training as a clinical intervention. In press, *Clinical Psychology: Science and Practice.*

Beck, D. & Cowen. C.C. (2006). *Spiral Dynamics: Mastering Values, Leadership and Change*. Malden, MA: Blackwell.

Bien, T., Bien, B. (2002). *Mindful Recovery: A Spiritual Path to Healing from Addiction.* New York: John Wiley & Sons, Inc.

Block, S. H., with Block, C. B. (2002). *Bridging the I-System: Unifying Spirituality and Behavior.* Ashland: White Cloud Press.

Block, S. H., and C. B. Block. (2007). *Come to Your Senses: Demystifying the Mind-Body Connection.* 2nd ed. New York: Atria Books/Beyond Words Publishing.

Block, S. H., and C. B. Block. (2010). *Mind-Body Workbook for PTSD: A 10-Week Program for Healing After Trauma.* Oakland, CA: New Harbinger Publications.

Block, S. H., and C. B. Block. (2012). *Mind-Body Workbook for Stress: Effective Tools for Lifelong Stress Reduction and Crisis Management.* Oakland, CA: New Harbinger Publications.

Block, S. H., and C. B. Block. (2013). *Mind-Body Workbook for Anger: Effective Tools for Anger Management and Conflict Resolution.* Oakland, CA: New Harbinger Publications.

Block, S. H., and C. B. Block. 2014. *Mind-Body Workbook for Anxiety: Effective Tools for Overcoming Panic, Fear and Worry.* Oakland, CA: New Harbinger Publications.

Blum, K. (1995). Reward deficiency syndrome: Electro-physiological and biogenetic evidence. Paper presented at the annual meeting of the Society for the Study of Neuronal Regulation, Scottsdale, AZ, April 15th.

Bly, R. (2001). *Iron John: Men and Masculinity.* London: Rider.

Boss, M. (1983). *The Existential Foundations of Medicine and Psychology.* New York: Jason Aronson.

Bourne, E. & Fox, R. (1973). *Alcoholism: Progress in Research & Treatment.* New York: Academic Press.

Bradshaw, J. (1998). *Healing the Shame that Binds You.* Florida: Health Communications Inc.

Brick, J. & Erickson, C. (1999) *Drugs, the Brain and Behavior: The pharmacology of Abuse and Dependence.* NY: Haworth Medical Press, Inc.

Calleja, D. (2011). Integral therapeutic community: A framework for adolescent addiction treatment. *Journal of Integral Theory and Practice*, 6(4): 93-112.

Campbell, J. (2004). *The Hero with a Thousand Faces.* New Jersey: Princeton University Press.

Camus, A. (2005). *The Myth of Sisyphus.* London: Penguin Books.

Carnes, P. (2008). *Facing the Shadow: Starting Sexual and Relationship Recovery*. Carefree, AZ: Gentle Path Press.

Carnes, P. (2001). *Out of the Shadows: Understanding Sexual Addiction*. Minnesota: Hazelden.

Carnes, P. (2008). *Recovery Start Kit*. Arizona: Gentle Path Press.

Carnes, P. (2009). *Recovery Zone Volume 1: Making Changes That Last: The Internal Tasks*. Minnesota: Carefree, AZ: Gentle Path Press.

Carnes, P., Laaser, D., Laaser, M. (1999). *Open Hearts: Renewing Relationships with Recovery, Romance, and Reality*. Carefree, AZ: Gentle Path Press.

Cook, C. H. (1998). The Minnesota Model in the management of drug and alcohol dependency: Miracle, method or myth? Part 2: Evidence and conclusions. *British Journal of Addiction*, 83, 735–748.

Cook-Greuter, S. R. (2004). Making the case for a developmental perspective, *Industrial and Commercial Training*, Vol. 36, No. 7. Emerald Group Publishing Limited.

Dayton, T. (2000). *Trauma and Addiction: Ending the Cycle of Pain Through Emotional Literacy*. Florida: Health Communications Inc.

DiClemente, C.C. (2003). *Addiction and Change: How Addictions Develop and Addicted People Recover*. New York: Guilford Press.

DiClemente, C.C. & Prochaska, J.O. (1998). Toward a comprehensive, transtheoretical model of change: Stages of change and addictive behaviors. In W. R. Miller & N. Heather (Eds.), *Treating addictive behaviors* (2nd ed., pp. 3-24). New York: Plenum Press.

Dick, P. K. (1977). *A Scanner Darkly*. Vintage Books: New York.

Duffett, L. (2010). Outcomes-based evaluative research at an integrally informed substance abuse treatment center using the Integrated Recovery model [unpublished thesis]. University of Cape Town, Department of Psychology.

Du Plessis, G.P. (2010). The integrated recovery model for addiction treatment and recovery. *Journal of Integral Theory and Practice*, 5(3), 68-87.

Du Plessis, G.P. (2012a). Integrated recovery therapy: Toward an integrally informed individual psychotherapy for addicted populations. *Journal of Integral Theory and Practice*, 7(1), 124-148.

Du Plessis, G.P. (2012b). Toward an integral model of addiction: By means of integral methodological pluralism as a metatheoretical and integrative conceptual framework. *Journal of Integral Theory and Practice*, 7(3), 1-24.

Du Plessis, G. P. (2013). The Import of Integral Pluralism in Striving Towards an Integral Metatheory of Addiction. Paper presented at the third biennial Integral Theory Conference, San Fransisco, CA, July 20, 2013.

Du Plessis, G. P. (2014). Towards an Integral Meta-theory of Addiction. MA dissertation at the University of South Africa.

Dupuy, J. (2013). *Integral Recovery: A Revolutionary Approach to the Treatment of Alcoholism and Addiction*: SUNY Press: New York.

Dupuy, J. & Gorman, A. (2010). Integral Recovery: An AQAL approach to inpatient alchohol and drug treatment, *Journal of Integral Theory and Practice*, 5(3), 86-101.

Dupuy, J., & Morelli, M. (2007). Toward an integral recovery model for drug and alcohol addiction. *AQAL: Journal of Integral Theory and Practice*, 2(3), 26-42.

Drever, J. (1989). *A Dictionary of Psychology*. Great Britain: Hazell Watson and Viney Ltd.

Eng, P. A. (2014). Piercing the Veil of Learned Helplessness: An integrated transpersonal model of addiction. PhD thesis at the California Institute of Integral Studies.

Erickson, C.K. (1989). Reviews and comments on alcohol research relaxation therapy, and endorphins in alcoholics. *Alcoholism*, 6, 525—526.

Esbjörn-Hargens, S. (2006). Integral research: A multi-method approach to investigating phenomena. *Constructivism and the Human Sciences*, 11(1), 79-107.

Esbjörn-Hargens, S. (2009). An overview of integral theory: An all-inclusive framework for the 21st century (Resource Paper No. 1). Boulder, CO: Integral Institute.

Esbjörn-Hargens, S. & Zimmerman. M. E. (2009). *Integral ecology: Uniting multiple perspectives on the natural world*. New York: Integral Books.

Fahrion, S., (Speaker). (1995) ISSSEEM Presidential Address: Human potential & Recordings.

Flores, P.J. (1997). *Group Psychotherapy with Addicted Populations*. Binghamton: The Haworth Press Inc.

Forman, M. (2010). *A Guide to Integral Psychotherapy:*

Complexity, Integration, and Spirituality in Practice. New York: SUNY Press.

Fox, K. J. (1999). Ideological implications of addiction theories and treatment. *Deviant Behavior: An Interdisciplinary Journal,* 20, 209-232.

Frankl, V. E. (1965). *The Doctor and the Soul*. Great Britain: Penguin Books.

Fromm, E. (1987). *The Art of Loving*. London: Unwin Paperbacks.

Gorman, A. (2013). Integral Recovery: A Case Study of an AQAL [All-quadrants, All-levels, All-lines, All-states, All-types] Approach to Addiction Treatment. PhD thesis at JFK University.

Hagen, S. (1997). *Buddhism Plain and Simple*. New York: Broadway Books.

Happold, F. C. (1975). *Mysticism: A Study and Anthology*. Great Britain: Penguin Books.

Harlowe, L., Newcomb, M., & Bentler, P. (1986). Depression, self-derogation, substance misuse and suicide ideation: Lack of purpose in life as a mediational factor. *Journal of Clinical Psychology*, 42:5-21.

Harris, B. (2004). *Thresholds of the Mind: Your Personal Roadmap to Success, Happiness and Contentment*. Oregon: Centerpointe Press.

Held, B. (2004) The negative side of positive psychology. *Journal of Humanistic Psychology*, Vol. 44 No.1, Winter, pp. 9-46.

Hesse, H. (1973). *Narziss and Goldmund.* London: Penguin Books.

Hesse, H. (1973). *Steppenwolf.* London: Penguin Books.

Hill, W. B. (2010). An ontological analysis of mainstream addiction theories: Exploring relational alternatives. Retrieved April 18, 2013 from http://search.proquest.com//docview/305185322.

Holford, P., Miller, D., & Braly, J. (2008). *How to Quit Without Feeling S**t.* Great Britain: Piatkus Books.

Ingersoll, R.E. & Zeitler, D.M. (2010). *Integral Psychotherapy: Inside Out/Outside In.* New York: SUNY Press.

Jacobson, G., Ritter, D., & Mueller, L. (1977). Purpose in life and personal values among adult alcoholics. *Journal of Clinical Psychology*, 33(1):314-316.

James, W. (1961/1901). *The Varieties of Religious Experience: A Study in Human Nature.* New York: Colliers.

Johnson, R. A. (1994). *Lying with the Heavenly Woman: Understanding and Integrating the Feminine Archetypes in Men's Lives.* NY: Harper Collins Publishers.

Jung, J. (2001). *Psychology of Alcohol and Other Drugs: A Research Perspective.* Thousand Oaks. CA: Sage Publications.

Kabat-Zinn, J. (1990). *Full Catastrophe Living: Using the Wisdom of Your Body and Mind to Face Stress, Pain, and Illness.* New York: Delacorte.

Kabat-Zinn, J. (1994). *Wherever You Go, There You Are: Mindfulness Meditation in Everyday Life.* New York: Hyperion.

Kabat-Zinn, J., Massion, M. D., Kristeller, J., Peterson, L.G., Fletcher, K.E., Pert, L., Lenderking, W.R., & Santorelli, S.F. (1992). Effectiveness of a meditation-based stress reduction program in the treatment of anxiety disorders. *American Journal of Psychiatry*, 149, 936–943.

Kernberg, O. F. (1975). *Borderline Conditions and Pathological Narcissism*. New York: Jason Aroson.

Khantzian, E.J. (1999). *Treating Addiction as a Human Process*. Northvale, NJ: Jason Aronson.

Khantzian, E.J., Halliday, K.S., & McAuliffe, W.E. (1990). *Addiction and the Vulnerable Self: Modified Dynamic Group Therapy for Substance Abusers*. New York: Guilford Press.

Kinnier, R., Metha, A., Keim, J., Okey, J., Adler-Tapia, R., Berry, M. & Mulvenon, S. (1994). Depression, meaninglessness, and substance abuse in "normal" and hospitalized adolescents. *Journal of Alcohol and Drug Education*, 39(2):101-111.

Kristeller, J.L. & Hallett, C.B. (1999). An exploratory study of a meditation-based intervention for binge eating disorder. *Journal of Health Psychology*, 4, 357–363.

Kohut, H. (1977). *The Restoration of Self*. New York: International University Press.

Kumar, S. M. (2002). An introduction to buddhism for the cognitive-behavioral therapist. *Journal of Cognitive and Behavioral Practice*, 9, (1), 47.

Kurtz, E. & Ketcham, K. (2002). *The Spirituality of Imperfection: Storytelling and the Search for Meaning*. New York: Bantam Books.

Laffaye, C., McKellar, J.D., Ilgen, M. A., & Moos, R. H. (2008). Predictors of 4-year outcome of community residential treatment for patients with substance use disorders. *Addictions*, 103, 67-680.

Laudet, Alexander B., Morgen, Keith, and White, William L. (2006). The role of social supports, spirituality, religiousness, life meaning and affiliation with Twelve-Step fellowship in quality of life satisfaction among individuals in recovery from alcohol and drug problems. *Alcoholism Treatment Quarterly*, 24 (1—2), 33–73.

Leonard, L. (1989). *Witness to the Fire: Creativity and the Veil of Addiction*. Boston: Shambhala.

Linehan, M. (1993). *Skill Training Manual for Treating Borderline Personality Disorder*. London: The Guilford Press.

Logsdon-Conradsen, S. (2002). Using mindfulness meditation to promote holistic health in individuals with HIV/AIDS. *Journal of Cognitive and Behavioral Practice,* 9, (1), 47.

Macquarrie, J. (1973). *Existentialism: An Introduction, Guide and Assessment*. London: Penguin Books.

Mahler, M.S., Pine, F. & Bergman, A. (1975). *The Psychological Birth of the Human Infant: Symbiosis and Individuation*. New York: Basic Books.

Marlatt, G. A. & Gordon, J. R. (1985). *Relapse Prevention: Maintenance Strategies in Treatment of Addictive Behaviors*. New York: Guilford Press.

Marlatt. G.A. (2002). Buddhist philosophy and the treatment of addictive behavior. *Journal of Cognitive and Behavioral Practice,* 9, (1), 47.

Marquis, A. (2008). *The Integral Intake: A Comprehensive Idiographic Assessment in Integral Psychotherapy.* New York: Taylor & Francis Group.

Max-Neef, M. A. with Antonio, E., & Hopenhayn, M. (1989). *Human Scale Development: Conception, Application and Further Reflections*. New York: Apex.

McPeak, J.D., Kennedy, B. P., & Gordon, S. M., (1991). Altered states of consciousness therapy: A missing component in alcohol and drug rehabilitation treatment. *Journal of Substance Abuse Treatment*, 8. 75-82.

Mellody, P., Miller, A.W., Miller, J.K. (1992). *Facing Love Addiction: Giving Yourself the Power to Change the Way You Love.* New York: HarperCollins.

Milkman, H.B. & Sunderwirth, S. G., (2010). *Craving for Ecstasy and Natural Highs: A Positive Approach to Mood Alteration.* CA: SAGE Publications Ltd.

Miller, W. R. (1998a). Researching the spiritual dimensions of alcohol and other drug problems. *Addiction*, 93(7): 979–90.

Miller W.R. (1998). Why do people change addictive behavior? *Addiction*, 93(2): 163–72.

Nakken, C.M. (1998). *Understanding the Addictive Process: Development of an Addictive Personality.* Hazelden: Hazelden Foundation.

Narcotics Anonymous World Services, Inc. (1993). *It Works: How and Why The Twelve Steps and Twelve Traditions.* Chatsworth, CA: Narcotics Anonymous World Services, Inc.

Narcotics Anonymous World Services, Inc. (1998). *The Narcotic Anonymous Step Working Guides.* Chatsworth, CA: Narcotics Anonymous World Services, Inc.

Narcotics Anonymous World Services, Inc. (2004). *Sponsorship.* Chatsworth, CA: Narcotics Anonymous World Services, Inc.

Nhat Hanh, T. (1987). *The Miracle of Mindfulness: An Introduction to the Practice of Meditation.* Boston: Beacon Press.

Nietzsche, F. (1980). *Thus Spoke Zarathustra.* Great Britain: Penguin Books.

Nixon, G. (2005). Beyond dry-drunkness: Facilitating second stage recovery using Wilber's "spectrum of consciousness developmental" model. *Journal of Social Work Practice in the Addictions*, 5(3), 55–71.

Nixon, G. (2013). *The Sun Rises in the Evening.* United Kingdom: Non-Duality Press.

Nixon, G. (2011). Transforming the addicted person's counterfeit quest for wholeness through three stages of recovery: A Wilber transpersonal spectrum of development clinical perspective. *International Journal of Mental Health and Addiction*, 1-21. Published online: November 24, 2011, 1-21. doi:10.1007/s11469-011-9365-y.

Nixon, G. (2001). Using Wilber's transpersonal model of psychological and spiritual growth in alcoholism treatment. *Alcoholism Treatment Quarterly*, 19(1), 79-95.

Peniston, E.G. (1994). EEG Alpha-theta Neurofeedback: Promising clinical approach for future psychotherapy and medicine. *Megabrain Report: The Journal of Optimal Performance*. 2, (4), 40-43.

Perlman, A. (2002). *Understanding.* Minnesota: Hazelden Foundation.

Perls, F. (1976). *The Gestalt Approach & Eye Witness to Therapy* (2nd ed.). New York: Bantam Books.

Peterson, C. & Seligman, M. E. P. (2004). *Character Strengths and Virtues: A Handbook and Classification.* Washington, DC: American Psychological Association.

Phillips, S. (2008). *Strength for Life.* New York: Ballantine Books.

Piaget, J. (1977). *The Essential Piaget*. H. E. Gruber & J. J. Voneche (Eds.). New York: Basic.

Prochaska, J.O. & DiClemente, C. C. (1992). Stages of change in the modification of problem behaviors. In: Hersen, M., Eisler, R.M., & Miller, P.M. (Eds.) *Progress in behavior modification*, Vol. 28 (184-214). Sycamore, IL: Sycamore Press.

Richo, D. (2002). *How to be an Adult in Relationships: The Five Keys to Mindful Loving.* Boston and London: Shambhala.

Rioux, D. (1996). Shamanic healing techniques: Toward holistic addiction counseling. *Alcoholism Treatment Quarterly*, 14(1), 59–69.

Ronell, A. (1993) *Crack Wars: Literature, Addiction, Mania.* Nebraska: University of Nebraska Press.

Rose, J.K. (2003). *The Joy Beyond Craving: A Buddhist Perspective on Addiction and Recovery.* Rio Roncho: Desert Wordsmith Productions.

Shealy, S.E. (2009). Toward an integrally informed approach to alcohol and drug treatment: Bridging the science-spirit gap. *Journal of Integral Theory and Practice*, 4(3), 109-126.

Siegel R. (1984). The natural history of hallucinogens. In Jacobs, B., editor. *Hallucinogens: Neurochemical, Behavioral and Clinical Perspectives*. New York: Raven Press.

Seligman, M. (2011). *Authentic Happiness: Using the New Positive Psychology to Realize Your Potential for Lasting Fulfillment*. Australia: Random House.

Seligman, M. (2012). *Flourish: A Visionary New Understanding of Happiness and Well-being.* New York: Free Press.

Seligman, M. E. P., Steen, T. A., Park, N. & Peterson, C. (2005). Positive psychology progress. *American Psychologist*, 60 (5), 410–421.

Schaeffer, B. (1997). *Is it Love or is it Addiction*. Minnesota: Hazelden.

Smuts, J.C. (1927). *Holism and Evolution* (2nd ed). London: Macmillan and Co.

Sobell, L., Ellingstad, T., Sobell, M. (2000). Natural recovery from alcohol and drug problems: Methodological review of the research and suggestions for future directions. *Addiction*, 95(5), 749–64.

Steiner, C. with Perry, P. (1997). *Achieving Emotional Literacy*. London: Bloomsbury.

Stone, H. & Stone, S. (1998) *Embracing Our Selves: The Voice Dialogue Manual*. Novato, CA: New World Library.

Tengan, A. (1999). *Search for Meaning as the Basic Human Motivation: A Critical Examination of Viktor Frankl's Logotherapeutic Concept of Man*. Frankfurt am Main: Lang.

Tolle, E. (2005). *A New Earth: Awakening to Your Life's Purpose.* London: Penguin Books.

Underhill, E. (1943). *Practical Mysticism*. New York: A Dutton Paperback.

Vogeler, C. (1969). *The Writers Journey: Mythic Structure for Writers* (2nd ed.). CA: Michael Wiese Productions.

Ulman, R.B. & Paul, H. (2006). *The Self Psychology of Addiction and its Treatment: Narcissus in Wonderland*. New York: Routledge.

Waisburg, J., & Porter, J. (1994). Purpose in life and outcomes of treatment for alcohol dependence. *British Journal of Clinical Psychology*, 33:49-63.

Weil, A., (1972). *The Natural Mind*. Boston: Houghton Mifflin.

White, W. L. (1996). *Pathways: From the Culture of Addiction to the Culture of Recovery*. Minnesota: Hazelden.

Whitfield, C.L. (1991). *Co-dependence: Healing the Human Condition*. Deerfield Beach: Health Communications Inc.

Wilber, K. (1997). An integral theory of consciousness. *Journal of Consciousness Studies*, 4 (1), 71–92.

Wilber, K. (2000). *Integral Psychology: Consciousness, Spirit, Psychology, Therapy*. Boston: Shambhala.

Wilber, K. (2006). *Integral Spirituality: A Startling New Role for Religion in the Modern and Postmodern World*. Boston: Integral Books.

Wilber, K. (1996). *A Brief History of Everything*. Boston & London: Shambhala.

Wilber, K. (2002). Excerpt A: An integral age at the leading edge. Retrieved May 9, 2011, from http://wilber.shambhala.com/html/books/kosmos/excerptA/excerptA.pdf.

Wilber, K. (2000). *Sex, Ecology, Spirituality: The Spirit of Evolution*. Boston: Shambhala.

Wilber, Ken (2004). *The Simple Feeling of Being*. Boston & London: Shambhala.

Wilber, K., Patten, T., Leonard, A. & Morelli, M. (2008). *Integral Life Practice: A 21st Century Blueprint for*

Physical Health, Emotional Balance, Mental Clarity, and Spiritual Awakening. Boston: Integral Books.

Winkelman, M. (2001). Alternative and traditional medicine approaches for substance abuse programs: A shamanic perspective. *International Journal of Drug Policy*, 12, 337-351.

Wilson, C. (1957). *The Outsider*. London: Victor Gollancz Ltd.

Yalom, I. (1980). *Existential Psychotherapy*. New York: Basic Books.

Yalom I. (1985). *The Theory and Practice of Group Psychotherapy* (4th ed). New York: Basic Books.

Zoja, L. (1989). *Drugs, Addiction and Initiation: The Modern Search for Ritual*. Boston: Sigo Press.

Tzu, Lao (Translated by James Legg). (2001). *Tao Te Ching*. United Kingdom: Axiom Publishing.

END NOTES:

1 Pinks, or *Wellconal,* is a synthetic opiate (Dipanone HCL) that was popular in the 1980s and early 1990s in South Africa, before heroin became freely available. *Wellconal* was manufactured as a painkiller to be taken orally but was primarily injected intravenously by drug users. The drug company GlaxoSmithKline SA (Pty) Ltd. manufactured the tablet in a bright pink color, filling the tablets with a large amount of chalk filler. What killed many users was the damage the chalk filler did to their heart and lungs. The average life expectancy of a *Pinks* user was between 2 to 5 years.

2 Dick, *A Scanner Darkly*, p. 180.

3 I am aware that any society, even ones operating from an Integral or worldcentric center of gravity, will also have pathology and developmentally arrested individuals, therefore addiction may, and probably will, always be present in any society, regardless of its developmental altitude. My opinion is that in more "enlightened" societies, addiction will not be as prevalent and take on the disastrous proportions it does in our contemporary society.

4 Wilber, *Sex, Ecology, Spirituality,* p. 541.

5 See Nixon, G. (2001). Using Wilber's transpersonal model of psychological and spiritual growth in alcoholism treatment. *Alcoholism Treatment Quarterly*, 19(1), 79-95. Nixon, G. (2005). Beyond dry-drunkness: Facilitating sec-

ond stage recovery using Wilber's "spectrum of consciousness developmental" model. *Journal of Social Work Practice in the Addictions*, 5(3), 55–71. Amodia, D. S., Cano, C., Eliason, M. J. (2005) An integral approach to substance abuse. *Journal of Psychoactive Drugs*. 37(4), 363-71. Dupuy, J., & Morelli, M. (2007). Toward an integral recovery model for drug and alcohol addiction. *AQAL: Journal of Integral Theory and Practice*, 2(3), 26-42. Shealy, S.E. (2009). Toward an integrally informed approach to alcohol and drug treatment: Bridging the science-spirit gap. *Journal of Integral Theory and Practice*, 4(3), 109-126. Du Plessis, G. P. (2010). Toward an integrated recovery model for drug and alcohol addiction. *AQAL: Journal of Integral Theory and Practice*, 5(3), 68-85. Dupuy, J., & Gorman, A. (2010). Integral recovery: An AQAL approach to inpatient alcohol and drug treatment. *AQAL: Journal of Integral Theory and Practice*, 5(3), 86-101. Calleja, D. (2011). Integral therapeutic community: A framework for adolescent addiction treatment. *Journal of Integral Theory and Practice*, 6(4):93-112. Nixon, G. (2011). Transforming the addicted person's counterfeit quest for wholeness through three stages of recovery: A Wilber transpersonal spectrum of development clinical perspective. *International Journal of Mental Health and Addiction*. 1-21. Published online: 24 November 2011, 1-21. doi:10.1007/s11469-011-9365-y. Du Plessis, G. P. (2012a). Integrated recovery therapy: Toward an integrally informed therapy for addicted populations. *AQAL: Journal of Integral Theory and Practice*, 7(1), 37-55. Du Plessis, G. P. (2012b). Toward an integral model of addiction: By means of integral methodological pluralism as a meta-theoretical and integrative conceptual framework. *AQAL: Journal of Integral Theory and Practice*, 7(2), 40-63. Dupuy, J. (2013). *Integral Recovery: A Revolutionary Approach to the Treatment of Alcoholism and Addiction*: SUNY Press: New York. Gorman, A. (2013), Integral Recovery: A Case Study of an AQAL [All-quadrants, All-levels, All-lines, All-states, All-types] Approach to Addiction Treatment. Phd thesis at JFK University. Du Plessis, G. P. (2014) Towards an Integral Meta-theory of Addiction. MA dissertation at the University of South Africa. Plessis, G. P. (2014): *A Integral Ontology of Addiction: A Multiple Object as a Continuum of Ontological Complexity. Journal of Integral Theory and Practice.* 9(1), 38-54.

6   Some of my personal "favorites" are (for humorous reasons) psychoanalyst Karl Abraham's theory on alcoholism—that it is a sexual perversion and indicative of forbidden repressed homosexual tendencies (I am sure this theory would not go down too well in AA meetings); and Edward Clover's theory that alcoholism stems from "oral rage" and "anal sadism." I shudder to think what their proposed "cures" for alcoholism would entail.

7   Quoted in Alcoholics Anonymous, *Big Book*, p. 570.

8   See the author's academic articles for a more in-depth discussion on the Integrated Recovery approach: Du Plessis, G.P. (2010). The Integrated Recovery Model for Addiction Treatment and Recovery. *Journal of Integral*

Theory and Practice, 5(3), 68-87. Du Plessis, G.P. (2012a). Integrated recovery therapy: Toward an integrally informed individual psychotherapy for addicted populations. *Journal of Integral Theory and Practice*, 7(1), 124-148. Du Plessis, G.P. (2012b). Toward an integral model of addiction: By means of integral methodological pluralism as a metatheoretical and integrative conceptual framework. *Journal of Integral Theory and Practice*, 7(3), 1-24. Du Plessis, G. P. (2013). The Import of Integral Pluralism in Striving Towards an Integral Metatheory of Addiction. Paper presented at the third biennial Integral Theory Conference, San Francisco, CA, July 20, 2013. Du Plessis, G. P. (2014): *A Integral Ontology of Addiction: A Multiple Object as a Continuum of Ontological Complexity. Journal of Integral Theory and Practice.* 9(1), 38-54. Anyone who would like a copy of these articles can contact the author at guy@guyduplessis.com.

9   Marquis, *The Integral Intake: A Comprehensive Idiographic Assessment in Integral Psychotherapy,* p. 23.

10   This chapter is based on my academic article *Du Plessis, G.P. (2010). The Integrated Recovery Model for Addiction Treatment and Recovery. Journal of Integral Theory and Practice, 5(3), 68-87.*

11   Esbjörn-Hargens, *An Overview of Integral Theory,* p. 2.

12   Image courtesy of Integral Institute.

13   See Brick, J. & Erickson, C. (1999). *Drugs, the Brain and Behavior: The Pharmacology of Abuse and Dependence.* NY: Haworth Medical Press, Inc.

14   Patrick Holford writes about reward deficiency as originated by Kenneth Blum.

15   See Erickson, C.K. (1989). Reviews and comments on alcohol research, relaxation therapy, and endorphins in alcoholics. *Alcoholism, 6,* 525-526.

16   See Flores, P.J. (1997). *Group psychotherapy with addicted populations.* Binghamton: The Haworth Press Inc.

17   White, *Pathways: From the Culture of Addiction to the Culture of Recovery,* pp. xxiii – xxiv.

18   Quoted in White, *Pathways: From the Culture of Addiction to the Culture of Recovery,* p. 1.

19   White, *Pathways: From the Culture of Addiction to the Culture of Recovery,* p. xxvii.

20   This becomes even more apparent when we explore the phenomenon with an understanding of Wilber's developmental stages. As addicts move from the egocentric stages of addiction to the ethnocentric stages of early recovery, they enter a stage of development where their "group" or "clan" plays a major role in healthy development and integration. More on this topic in the chapter about the social recovery dimension.

21   See the work of Howard Gardner on multiple intelligences.

22   In working with addicted patients at various stages of their recovery, and in trying to apply the psychograph model to their processes, the author noted that what would be referred to as "healthy" emotional development for somebody with a month of clean time, i.e. a month free of acting on the addiction, would be considered "unhealthy" development for somebody with ten years of clean time. (In the same way that receiving 50% for Grade 1 reading skills is acceptable when you are eight years old, but problematic if you are 25 years old.) Using a standard developmental model and psychograph, one could easily arrive at the conclusion that somebody in early recovery has "low" emotional development and somebody with ten years clean has "higher" emotional development. This type of "scoring" is not useful and does not take into account what healthy emotional development should look like at different stages. Therefore, what would score "high" on a psychograph of an individual with a month of clean time would score "low" on a psychograph for an individual with ten years of clean time. This means that for each stage of development, an "independent" psychograph needs to be developed.

23   Wilber, *Integral Spirituality,* p. 5.

24   Dupuy, *Integral Recovery*, p. 41

25   Image courtesy of Integral Institute.

26   This image is Creative Commons, designed by Guy du Plessis.

27   See Nixon, G. (2011). Transforming the addicted person's counterfeit quest for wholeness through three stages of recovery: A Wilber transpersonal spectrum of development clinical perspective. *International Journal of Mental Health and Addiction*, 1-21.

28   See McPeake et al., 1991.

29   See McPeake et al. 1991; Weil, 1972; Winkelman, 2001; Ken Wilber, personal communication, January 13, 2011.

30   Winkelman, Alternative and traditional medicine approaches for substance abuse programs: A shamanic perspective. *International Journal of Drug Policy*, 12, pp. 338 – 339.

31   Milkman & Sunderwirth, *Craving for Ecstasy and Natural Highs: A Positive Approach to Mood Alteration*, p. 6.

32   Milkman & Sunderwirth, *Craving for Ecstasy and Natural Highs: A Positive Approach to Mood Alteration*, p.19.

33   Alcoholics Anonymous, *Twelve Steps and Twelve Traditions*, p. 106.

34   Esbjörn-Hargens, *An Overview of Integral Theory*, p. 15.

35   This image is Creative Commons, designed by Guy du Plessis.

36   Dupuy, Toward an integral recovery model for drug and alcohol addiction. *Journal of Integral Theory and Practice*, p. 37.

37   Obviously many addicts suffer from both masculine and feminine voice pathologies and addictions, yet most will have a tendency to lean more towards one side of the masculine/feminine addiction continuum, or certain environments will activate a certain pathological voice. This concept is meant to be used as a general orienting framework, not as an exact diagnostic tool.

38   Wilber, Excerpt A, www.kenwilber.com, p. 98

39   Kabat-Zinn, *Wherever You Go There You Are,* pp. 3-4.

40   See Blum, K. (1995). Reward deficiency syndrome: Electro-physiological and biogenetic evidence. Paper presented at the annual meeting of the Society for the Study of Neuronal Regulation, Scottsdale, AZ, April 15.

41   Perls, *The Gestalt Approach & Eye Witness to Therapy,* p. 66.

42   Perls, *Gestalt Approach & Eye Witness to Therapy,* p. 63.

43   This image is Creative Commons, designed by Guy du Plessis.

44   Narcotics Anonymous World Services, Inc (1988). *Narcotics Anonymous*, CA. p. 45.

45   It is worth mentioning that initially, when an individual starts meditating, matters can get worse. The powerful, instinctive, addictive patterns may reassert themselves with a vengeance and may put up a desperate fight. In meditation,

the contents of the unconscious come to the surface and agitate consciousness. Jung called this repressed, unconscious material the shadow; and the initial stages of meditation, like in therapy and early recovery, often bring about an experience of *Nigredo* (the alchemical term which describes the first stage of the alchemical Opus, characterized by passion, depression, disorientation, and dissolution). When the individual persists through this dark night of the soul, things eventually begin to quiet down. Then feelings of serenity and inner peace may become part of the personality. The Integrated Recovery approach focuses primarily, but not exclusively, on mindfulness meditation methods. For addicts with psychotic disorders or those with a pre-Oedipal fault line in their personality structure, the practice of meditation may be counterproductive until their basic ego structure is fairly solid. It is therefore advised for addicts of this type who are in early recovery to seek advice from their therapist or counselor before a formal daily meditative practice is pursued.

46   Block, *Bridging the I-System*, p. 88.

47   Thoreau in Kabat-Zinn, *Wherever You Go There You Are*, p. 1.

48   Nietzsche, *Thus Spoke Zarathustra*, p. 288.

49   Seligman et al., Positive Psychology Progress, *American Psychologist*, p. 410.

50   See Laudet, Alexander B., Morgen, Keith, & White, William L. (2006). The role of social supports, spirituality, religiousness, life meaning, and affiliation with Twelve-Step fellowship in quality of life satisfaction among individuals in recovery from alcohol and drug problems. *Alcoholism Treatment Quarterly*, 24 (1—2), 33–73.

51   Seligman et al., Positive Psychology Progress, *American Psychologist*, p. 411.

52   Seligman et al., Positive Psychology Progress, *American Psychologist*, p. 412.

53   To find out your signature strengths, go to Seligman's website www. authentichappiness.org and take the VIA Strengths Survey.

54   Smuts, General, the Right Hon. J. C. (1926). *Holism and Evolution*. London: Macmillan, p. 312.

55   Ulman & Paul, *The Self Psychology of Addiction and its Treatment*, p. 6.

56   Flores, *Group Psychotherapy with Addicted Populations,* p. 278.

57   Ibid., p. 280.

58   Ibid., p. 280.

59   See Manfred A. Max-Neef with Antonio Elizalde, Martin Hopenhayn. (1989). *Human Scale Development: Conception, Application and Further Reflections*. New York: Apex. Chpt. 2. "Development and Human Needs." Max-Neef sees basic human needs as ontological (stemming from the condition of being human) and in many ways opposes the hierarchical needs model of thinkers like Maslow. I belive that Max-Neef's work on human needs is very applicable when understanding addiction from a needs perpective.

60   See Bourne, E. & Fox, R. (1973). *Alcoholism: Progress in Research & Treatment*. New York: Academic Press. Laudet, A.B., Morgen, K. & White, W.L. (2006). The role of social supports, spirituality, religiousness, life meaning and affiliation with 12-Step fellowship in quality of life satisfaction among individuals in recovery from alcohol and drug problems. *Alcoholism Treatment Quarterly, 24*(1-2), 33-73. Laffaye, C., McKellar, J.D., Ilgen, M. A., & Moos, R. H. (2008). Predictors of 4-year outcome of community residential treatment for patients with substance use disorders. *Addictions,* 103, 67-680.

61   Kurtz & Ketcham, *The Spirituality of Perfection: Storytelling and the Search for Meaning*, p. 4.

62   See Laudet, Alexander B.; Morgen, Keith and White, William L. (2006). The role of social supports, spirituality, religiousness, life meaning and affiliation with Twelve-Step fellowship in quality of life satisfaction among individuals in recovery from alcohol and drug problems. *Alcoholism Treatment Quarterly*, 24 (1—2), 33–73.

63   See Laffaye, C., McKellar, J.D., Ilgen, M. A., & Moos, R. H. (2008). Predictors of 4-year outcome of community residential treatment for patients with substance use disorders. *Addictions*, 103, 67-680.

64   Flores, *Group Psychotherapy with Addicted Populations,* p. 249.

65   Holford et al., *How to Quit without Feeling S**T*, p. 50.

66   Most of the information and suggestions in this chapter are derived from Holford, P., Miller, D., & Braly, J. (2008). *How to Quit Without Feeling S**T.* Great Britain: Piatkus Books.

67   Holford et al., *How to Quit without Feeling S**T*, p. 57.

68   See Holford et al., *How to Quit without Feeling S**T.*

69   See Holford et al., *How to Quit without Feeling S**T.*

70   See A. E. Abrahamson & A.W. Pezet, *Body, Mind and Sugar*. New York, Pyramid Books, 1976.

71   For more information on the FIT technique, check out Shawn Phillips' book *Strength for Life* or the Body module in the book *Integral Life Practice* for an in-depth discussion of this technique.

72   Wilber et. al., *Integral Life Practice*, p. 152.

73   Success rate measured by addicts who stayed clean up to three years after receiving the Peniston protocol.

74   See Peniston, E.G. (1994). EEG Alpha-theta Neurofeedback: Promising clinical approach for future psychotherapy and medicine. *Megabrain Report: The Journal of Optimal Performance.* 2, (4), 40-43.

75   See Erickson, C.K. (1989). Reviews and comments on alcohol research relaxation therapy, and endorphins in alcoholics, *Alcoholism.* 6, 525—526.

76   Flores, *Group Psychotherapy with Addicted Populations,* pp. 252-253.

77   Steve Hagen, *Buddhism Plain and Simple*, p. 69.

78   Alcoholics Anonymous, *Big Book*, p. 48.

79   Lao Tzu (Translated by James Legge), *Tao Te Ching*, pp. 9, 11.

80   Bradshaw, *Healing the Shame that Binds You*, p. 161.

81   Bradshaw, *Healing the Shame that Binds You*, p. 161.

82   Ibid., p. 161.

83   Ibid., p. 161.

84   Ibid., p. 165.

85   Ibid., p. 165.

86   Tompkins in Dayton, *Trauma and Addiction*, p. xiv.

87   Ibid., p. xiv.

88   Perls, *The Gestalt Approach & Eye Witness to Therapy,* p. 85.

89   Khantzian in Flores, *Group Psychotherapy with Addicted Populations,* p. 208.

90   Understanding this mechanism could point out why many heroin addicts have dysfunctional bonds with their mothers. From this perspective, heroin use can be understood as a pseudo-chemical substitute for this "mother-infant" bond that never was. That is why heroin addicts often cross-addict to romantic relationships that offer a similar chemical reward. And this is why many heroin addicts have relapsed when in failed romantic relationships in early recovery—it reactivates the original wounding. This phenomenon is not unique to heroin addicts but very common in this particular drug population.

91   Dayton, *Trauma and Addiction,* p. xix.

92   Pert, in Dayton, T., *Trauma and Addiction,* p. 6.

93   Dayton, *Trauma and Addiction,* p. 17.

94   Van der Kolk, in Dayton, *Trauma and Addiction,* p. 20.

95   Ibid., p. 18.

96   Flores, *Group Psychotherapy with Addicted Populations,* pp. 232-233.

97   Dayton, *Trauma and Addiction,* p. 18.

98   "Emotional literacy is made up of 'the ability to understand your emotions, the ability to listen to others and empathize with their emotions, and the ability to express emotions productively. To be emotionally literate is to be able to handle emotions in a way that improves your personal power and improves the quality of life around you. Emotional literacy improves relationships, creates loving possibilities between people, makes co-operative work possible, and facilitates the feeling of community." Steiner, C. with Perry, P. (1997). *Achieving Emotional Literacy.* London: Bloomsbury, pp. 11.

99   Alcoholics Anonymous World Services, Inc. Service material from the General Service Office.

100   Alcoholics Anonymous World Services, Inc. Service material from the General Service Office.

101   Leonard, *Witness to the Fire: Creativity and the Veil of Addiction*, p. 70.

102   Wilber et. al., *Integral Life Practice*, p. 50.

103   Ibid., p. 50.

104   I would not recommend using the 3-2-1 Shadow Process for issues that involve serious abuse. I do not believe that any shadow or forgiveness method that includes visualizing an abuser or speaking from the perspective of an abuser is beneficial.

105   Ibid., pp. 50-51.

106   Linehan, *Skills Training Manual for Treating Borderline Personality Disorder*, p. 1.

107   Linehan, *Skills Training Manual for Treating Borderline Personality Disorder*.

108   Perlman, *Understanding*, p. 1.

109   Wilber in Marquis, *The Integral Intake: A Comprehensive Idiographic Assessment in Integral Psychotherapy*, p. 87.

110   Whitfield, *Co-dependence: Healing the Human Condition*, p. 53.

111   Zoja, *Drugs, Addiction and Initiation: The Modern Search for Ritual*, p. 58.

112   Frankl in Tengan, 1999, *Search for Meaning as the Basic Human Motivation*, p. 142.

113   Yalom, 1980, *Existential Psychotherapy*, p. 422.

114   Nietzsche in Frankl, 1984, p. 97.

115   See Kinnier, R., Metha, A., Keim, J., Okey, J., Adler-Tapia, R., Berry, M. & Mulvenon, S. (1994). Depression, meaninglessness, and substance abuse in "normal" and hospitalized adolescents. *Journal of Alcohol and Drug Education*, 39(2):101-111.

116   Harlowe, L., Newcomb, M., & Bentler, P. (1986). Depression, self-derogation, substance misuse and suicide ideation: Lack of purpose in life as a mediational factor. *Journal of Clinical Psychology*, 42:5-21.; and Jacobson,

G., Ritter, D., & Mueller, L. (1977). Purpose in life and personal values among adult alcoholics. *Journal of Clinical Psychology,* 33(1):314-316.

117   See Waisburg, J., & Porter, J. (1994). Purpose in life and outcomes of treatment for alcohol dependence. *British Journal of Clinical Psychology*, 33:49-63.

118   Wilber et. al., *Integral Life Practice*, pp. 373, 374.

119   Wilber et. al., *Integral Life Practice*, p. 379.

120   In Nietzsche, *Thus Spoke Zarathustra*, p. 30.

121   Frankl, *The Doctor and the Soul*, p. 12.

122   Frankl, *The Doctor and the Soul*, p. 12.

123   Leonard, L., *Witness to the Fire: Creativity and the Veil of Addiction*, p. 48.

124   James in Flores, *Group Psychotherapy with Addicted Populations*, p. 263.

125   Bill W. (Bill Wilson), co-founder of Alcoholics Anonymous.

126   Tolle, *A New Earth,* p. 301.

127   Wilber, *Integral Spirituality*, p. 100.

128   See Winkelman, M. (2001). Alternative and traditional medicine approaches for substance abuse programs: A shamanic perspective. *International Journal of Drug Policy*, 12, 337-351.

129   Zoja, *Drugs, Addiction and Initiation: The Modern Search for Ritual,* p. 93.

130   Ronell, *Crack Wars*, p. 103.

131   Winkelman, Alternative and traditional medicine approaches for substance abuse programs: A shamanic perspective. *International Journal of Drug Policy*, 12, 337-351, p. 340.

132   See McPeake et al. in Winkelman, Alternative and traditional medicine approaches for substance abuse programs: A shamanic perspective. *International Journal of Drug Policy*, 337-351.

133   From website http://www.addictionintegratedrecovery.weebly.com

134   This image is Creative Commons, designed by Guy du Plessis.

135   Although I do believe that in order for fellowships like AA and NA to stay relevant with the times, they have to adjust themselves to the dominant culture, I am aware that I am running the risk of being accused of "blasphemy" by saying this in certain circles. A good start might be to replace some of their terminology to make it more culturally relevant for today. It is unfortunate that the *Big Book* of AA is sometimes treated as if it is "divinely inspired." Why has the basic text of AA's *Big Book* not been changed since its inception? It is obvious that a manuscript written in 1933 will eventually become outdated in future cultures and, if not updated, will become linguistically inaccessible. I personally like the floral and dramatic tone of the *Big Book*, but many do not. Many, including myself, are also uncomfortable with the Judeo-Christian and patriarchical terminology often used. For 12-step fellowships to remain relevant in our rapidly changing world, its texts need to be accessible to the majority of the individuals whom it appeals to. I am sure Bill W. would be the first to change the basic text of AA, if he felt it was not serving its purpose as well as it could.

136   I know I am running the risk of being accused of all sorts of bad things by postmodernists and eco-feminists for saying one belief or culture is better than the other. I am actually not saying it is better—merely that one is higher on a scale of evolutionary development. Moreover, I am not saying that a person who believes in a mythic religion is wrong and cannot get recovery. What I am saying is that I take offense when somebody imposes a mythic belief on me, especially if he wants to burn me at the stake or blow me up because I disagree with his mythic beliefs.

137   Wilber, *Integral Spirituality: A Startling New Role for Religion in the Modern and Postmodern World,* p. 93.

138   Image courtesy of Shambhala Publications.

139   Mountain, *The Joy Beyond Craving: A Buddhist Perspective on Addiction and Recovery*, p. 112.

140   Alcoholics Anonymous, *Big Book*, p. 85.

141   Wilber, *Integral Spirituality: A Startling New Role for Religion in the Modern and Postmodern World,* p. 197.

142   Wilber, *Sex Ecology, Spirituality,* p. 236.

143   Ibid., p. 236.

144   Ibid., p. 236.

145   Ibid., p. 307.

146   Wilber et. al., *Integral Life Practice*, pp. 237-238.

147   See http://www.iAwake Technologies.com.

148   Below is a summary of some characteristics of each of these brainwave states:

Beta (14-30 Hz)
Mental: Daily thinking mind, arousal, alertness, cognition. Higher levels of beta waves are associated with anxiety, unease, feelings of separation, a strong sense of "me," self protection, indulgence, fear, anger, depression. Time seems to move faster.
Neuronal: Activates the sympathetic nervous system: "fight, flight, or freeze."
Chemical / Hormonal: Cortisol production. Cortisol is a hormone that is naturally produced by the adrenal glands. Cortisol is the major age-accelerating hormone within the brain. It also interferes with learning and memory and is, in general, bad news for your health and well-being.

Alpha (8-13.9 Hz)
Mental: Relaxation, super-learning, relaxed focus, light trance, pre-waking, meditative, beginning of access to unconscious mind, increased creativity. Time slows down.
Neuronal: Activates the parasympathetic nervous system: reduced heart rate and blood pressure, relaxed muscles, and increased percentage of oxygen flow to the brain. Pre-sleep, improved digestion, and nutrient assimilation.
Chemical / Hormonal: Serotonin is a chemical messenger that increases relaxation and eases pain. Endorphins are released when the brain is exposed to alpha and theta binaural beat patterns, enhancing many mental functions. Endorphins have a powerful strengthening effect on learning and memory. DHEA levels are a key determinant of physiological age and resistance to disease. Melatonin is a hormone that helps to create restful sleep. We make less of it as we age, and since during sleep many important rejuvenating substances are created in the brain, the inability to sleep soundly can dramatically decrease the quality of your life and greatly accelerate the aging process.

Theta (4-7.9 Hz)

Mental: Dreaming (lucid or sleeping), REM sleep, creative flow, integrative, emotional experiences, potential change in behavior, increased retention of learned material, hypnagogic imagery, trance, deep meditation, access to unconscious mind and intuition, increased creative potential, and spontaneous insight. Time slows down.
Chemical / Hormonal: Catecholamines, acetylcholine, vasopressin: these are vital for intelligence, memory, and learning, staving off Alzheimer's and other conditions involving memory loss. They increase our access to memories and boost creativity. Serotonin, endorphins, DHEA, melatonin: see under alpha.

Delta (.1-3.9 Hz)
Mental: Dreamless (lucid or sleeping), deep, trance-like, non-physical state, body awareness—including time and space—is limited to non-existent. Access to unconscious and "collective unconscious" mind. Time seems to stand still.
Chemical / Hormonal: Human growth hormone: HGH decreases body fat, increases muscle mass, increases bone density, increases energy levels, improves skin tone and texture, and improves immune system function.

149   Dupuy, J. (2007). Toward an integral recovery model for drug and alcohol addiction. *Journal of Integral Theory and Practice*, 2 (3), 26–42. p. 32.

150   Wilber et. al., *Integral Life Practice*, p. 217.

151   Ibid., p. 276.

152   Narcotics Anonymous World Services, *It Works: How and Why*, p. 111.

153   Wilber et. al., *Integral Life Practice*, p. 217.

154   Zoja, *Drugs, Addiction and Initiation: The Modern Search for Ritual* , p. 15.

155   White, *Pathways: From the Culture of Addiction to the Culture of Recovery*, p. 5.

156   Fromm, *The Art of Loving*, p. 109.

157   Khantzian in Flores, *Group Psychotherapy with Addicted Populations,* p. 208.

158   Flores, *Group Psychotherapy with Addicted Populations,* p. 245.

159   White, *Pathways: From the Culture of Addiction to the Culture of Recovery*, p. 255.

160   White, *Pathways: From Culture of Addiction to the Culture of Recovery*, p. 255.

161   White, *Pathways: From the Culture of Addiction to the Culture of Recovery*, pp. 222-223.

162   Flores, *Group Psychotherapy with Addicted Populations,* p. 9.

163   Zoja, *Drugs Addiction and Initiation: The Modern Search for Ritual,* pp. 12-13.

164   Zoja, *Drugs, Addiction and Initiation: The Modern Search for Ritual,* pp. 12-13.

165   White, *Pathways: From the Culture of Addiction to the Culture of Recovery*, p. 173.

166   Narcotics Anonymous World Services, Inc. (2004) *Sponsorship.* Chatsworth, CA: Narcotics Anonymous World Services, Inc.

167   Johnson, *Lying with the Heavenly Woman: Understanding and Integrating the Feminine Archetypes in Men's Lives,* pp. 18-19.

168   Johnson, *Lying with the Heavenly Woman: Understanding and Integrating the Feminine Archetypes in Men's Lives,* pp. 18-19.

169   Fromm, *The Art of Loving*, p. 42.

170   Flores, *Group Psychotherapy with Addicted Populations,* p. 438.

171   Donne in Kabat-Zinn, *Wherever You Go There You Are,* p.162.

172   Wei Wu Wei in Wilber, *Simple Feeling of Being,* p. 125.

173   From website retrieved on the 25th of June, 2010. http://www.integrityvikingfunds.com/PortalIntegrityFunds/DesktopModules/ViewDocument.aspx?DocumentID=456

174   From website retrieved on the 26th of June, 2010, http://www.cosmicharmony.com/Ia/SacredPl/Sacred6.htm.

175   Wilber et. al., *Integral Life Practice*, p. 296.

176   Although I prefer Max-Neef's approach to the nature of human needs, Maslow's model is useful for explaining the premise of this chapter. Although Max-Neef's needs model is non-hierarchical, he also acknowledges that if basic subsistency needs (which in many ways correlate with the first two levels of Maslow's model) are not met, it can compromise the whole needs system.

177   Perls, *The Gestalt Approach & Eye Witness to Therapy*, p. 9.

178   LoPorto, *The DaVinci Method: Break Out & Express Your Fire*, p. 110.

179   LoPorto, *The DaVinci Method: Break Out & Express Your Fire*, p. 109.

180   Kurtz & Ketcham, *The Spirituality of Perfection: Storytelling and the Search for Meaning*, p. 159.

181   The clinical applications of this method is called Integrated Recovery Therapy (IRT) and Integrated Recovery Coaching (IRC). IRT is a "meta-therapy" in the sense that it provides a multiperspectival and meta-theoretical perspective of the therapeutic process when guiding addicted clients in their recovery process. See my article: Du Plessis, G.P. (2012a). Integrated Recovery Therapy: Toward an integrally informed individual psychotherapy for addicted populations. *Journal of Integral Theory and Practice*, 7(1), 124-148.

182   These templates and an Integrated Recovery Workbook can be downloaded from my websites: www.integraladdictiontreatment.com and www.guyduplessis.com.

183   An Integgrated Recovery planner (IRP) planner and Integrated Recovery Wheel (IRW) are tools that provide an easily accessible, quantifiable and accountable "recovery structure" for both client and therapist to plan and guage the complex recovery process. These recovery tools also serve an underlying psychodynamic purpose for recovering addicts. Most addicts suffer from various degrees of pathological narcissism, which can be understood as the regression/fixation to the stage of the archaic, nuclear self. The narcissistically regressed/fixated individual often has a need for omnipotent control, a characteristic of the grandiose self. In active addiction, such power is sought through fusion with an omnipotent self-object (drug of choice), and manifests as impulsivity. Once in recovery, this need for control will initially manifest as obsessive compulsive personality traits of ritual and rigidity. Without some clear "recovery structure," and the absence of the previously idealized self-object (drug(s) of choice), the narcissistically regressed individual will be subject to massive anxiety, stemming from fear of fragmentation of self, and "empty" depression, which reflects the scantiness of psychic structure and good internal objects. The

structure of an IRP and IRW can help satisfy the need for ritual and rigidity in a healthy way, and once this "recovery structure" is internalized, it will help build much needed psychic structure.

184   Cook-Greuter, Making the case for a developmental perspective, *Industrial and Commercial Training*, Vol. 36 No. 7, 2004, Emerald Group Publishing Limited.

185   Max-Neef, M. A. with Antonio, E., & Hopenhayn, M. (1989). *Human Scale Development: Conception, Application and Further Reflections.* New York: Apex. p. 31.

186   This image is Creative Commons, designed by Guy du Plessis.

187   This image is Creative Commons, designed by Guy du Plessis.

188   I am thankfull to Peter Powis who introduced me to a similar excersice, which I adapted to create the STOP technique.

189   Nixon (2012), Transforming the addicted person's counterfeit quest for wholeness through three stages of recovery: AWilber transpersonal spectrum of development clinical perspective. *Int'l Journal of Mental Health Addiction,* 10:407–427, p. 425.

190   Nixon (2012), Transforming the addicted person's counterfeit quest for wholeness through three stages of recovery: AWilber transpersonal spectrum of development clinical perspective. *Int'l Journal of Mental Health Addiction,* 10:407–427, p. 425

191   See Gary Nixon's book *The Sun Rises in the Evening,* John Dupuy's book *Integral Recovery,* and Dr. Robert Weathers soon-to-be published book *Plural Recovery: Integrally Informed Therapy and Relapse Prevention for Couples.*

192   Stone & Stone, *Embracing Our Selves: The Voice Dialogue Manual*, pp. 87-88.

193   Block from website http://mindbodybridging.com/mind_body_bridging_what_is.htm.

194   From website http://mindbodybridging.com/mind_body_bridging_what_is.htm.

195   Image courtesy of Stanley H. Block, M.D.

196   From website www.mindbodybridging.com/ mind_body_bridging_ what_is.htm.

197   From website http//bridging theisystem.com/.

198   Personal communication with Stanley Block. 13 October 2014

199   For those interested in Mind-Body Bridging, I recommend reading Dr. Block's book *Come to Your Senses (2ⁿᵈ Ed.)*, *Mind-Body Workbook for PTSD, Mind-Body Workbook for Anxiety* or visit the website www.mindbodybridging. com.

CPSIA information can be obtained
at www.ICGtesting.com
Printed in the USA
BVHW052257261118
533946BV00003B/454/P